More Memories
of
Ipswich

The publishers would like to thank the following companies for their

support in the production of this book

Listers

Otley College

M W Partridge & Co Limited

A Soames & Sons

First published in Great Britain by True North Books Limited
England HX3 6AE
01422 344344

ISBN 1 903204 52 6

Text, design and origination by True North Books Limited
Printed and bound by The Amadeus Press Limited

More Memories of Ipswich

Contents

Introduction

Can you remember when we had snow in the winter, rain in the spring, sunshine in the summer and fog in the autumn, or is this something your parents told you about before our seasons seemed to merge? Are you of a generation that hankers for the days of Dan Dare in the 'Eagle', Stinker Murdoch in 'Much binding in the marsh' and Lita Roza warbling about that little doggie in the window? If so, this is the book for you. 'More Memories of Ipswich' makes no apologies for taking a nostalgic trip in time back to the middle of the last century when our hometown had such a different look and the pace of life was much more measured. We will see again the pleasures that could be gained from admitting to be a supporter of the royal family, of bringing the family saloon into the town centre and walking around it at night without the fear of being accosted by some lager swilling lout whose idea of a good time is to be as noisy and as obnoxious as possible. If you have forgotten those times, then these pages will help to rekindle the memories. The photographs have been carefully chosen to remind us of those days gone by and are pointed up by text that is a mixture of comment, factual description and amusing anecdote, all designed to capture the mood of the era.

It is sometimes said that nostalgics are people who only view the past with the benefit of their rose tinted glasses. That may have some element of truth, but inside these pages the reader will find that the difficult times have not

Soccer fans celebrate Ipswich Town's return to Division One in 1968.

been ignored. As well as pictures of celebration and fun there are some that will bring a tear to the eye as we relive the dark days of the war when the Heinkels and Junkers flew overhead and unleashed their cargoes of death and destruction upon our town. Not everything in our past is memorable for joyous reasons, but by recognising the pain we can better appreciate the warmth created by happy occasions. We can also learn from the past in our attempts to build a better future. Is our lifestyle better now than it was yesterday? It must be, as poverty, sickness and deprivation are nowhere near as common in the welfare state we have created that has brought us to a more stable and richer existence. Yet not everything changes for the better and 'More Memories of Ipswich' will help readers make up their own minds about which elements of our life that are no more can be regarded as a loss to society or merely a stage through which we had to grow.

Perhaps it is a good idea to get the children to sit down and leaf through the pages that follow and remind them of their heritage and the inheritance that we have created for them. To them the 1970s are olden times, so help them appreciate that to us that decade was the beginning of the modern era and is a time where this book finishes. Use the images within to help them better understand what it was like when their parents and grandparents were growing up. Point out the activities and pastimes we found so enjoyable when we were young and how we took a delight in creating some of own entertainment. Return them to an Ipswich that buzzed with activity in the Corn Exchange, the port was crowded with barges on their way to bring home the troops from Dunkirk, cars parked outside the Town Hall and we ate our first banana for years. These are the streets that gave Dickens his inspiration for 'Pickwick Papers', the thoroughfares that Gainsborough and Constable strode when they put their easels to one side for a while and the places where lived the characters that provided Giles with the basis for his humorous newspaper cartoons.

Ipswich is one of England's oldest towns and evidence of a Roman villa has been discovered near the northern boundary, though its true origins lie in the seventh century during Saxon times. The settlement of Gippeswyc, as it was known in medieval times, grew around a fordable spot on the River Orwell. The centre of population could be found on the line of what is now Westgate, Tavern Street and Carr Street. Even in those early days the town was a hive of industry with pottery being particularly important. Ipswich ware, to give it a modern spelling, was distinctive, being produced by the then advanced technique of using wheel-thrown clay that was then fired in a kiln. The

Shoppers on St Matthew's Street in December 1966.

town expanded under the control of the Wuffingas and its importance as an economic centre was illustrated by the number of people involved in the minting of coins. Suffolk was one of the most heavily populated areas of the country and Ipswich developed as a port of considerable influence, trading everyday goods alongside such luxury items as furs, fine wines and jewellery. Unfortunately its prosperity attracted the attention of the Vikings and the Danes who regarded the town as easy pickings. During the first part of the 11th century a heavy price was being paid to the assaults from across the water. The Norman Conquest of 1066 brought further strife and many profitable manses and burgesses were laid waste.

But, you cannot keep a good town down. Resilient Ipswich bounced back and was soon back to its position of significance as a major trading port, specialising in exports of wool, textiles and agricultural products from the 12th century to the end of the Tudor period. By then it had also gained a reputation as an embarkation platform to the new world as emigrants set off to the Americas to seek fame and fortune on the other side of the Atlantic. All this time Ipswich continued to act as a vibrant market town that served both its agricultural hinterland and that of the capital city to where food was transported along the coast. Yet there was a strange mixture of stagnation and growth during the 18th century, the former being largely due to the silting up of the Orwell that restricted the size of vessels able to access the port. It was the coming of the Industrial Revolution that helped to kickstart the town's prosperity once more. For the first time anywhere a steam dredger was used to help clear the river and the then world's largest wet dock was constructed in the 1840s. Ipswich was reborn.

During the 20th century light engineering became important to the economy and these days Ipswich still prospers as a major agricultural market and service centre for the extensive and rich farming area of Suffolk. It is to the middle period of that century that 'More Memories of Ipswich' will now take you. It was an age when Brownies wore berets instead of baseball caps, little boys had chapped knees, you could call someone a housewife without giving offence and drink beer from a glass instead of directly from a bottle. To help you get in the right mood for the nostalgic experience of a lifetime why not discard the mobile phone and press button A to connect instead? Reach for a packet of Spangles and suck away happily as you enjoy the music of Dickie Valentine crooning on an old 78. Chuckle to the quips of Julian and Sandy in 'Round the Horne' on the wireless and light up a Craven A as you recall William Boyd as Hopalong Cassidy riding into town on Topper.

Street scenes

Pedestrians move freely along here nowadays since motor vehicles were forbidden access, though they can still drive across on Northgate Street and Upper Brook Street to the right and left. The cyclist was about to cross from Carr Street into Tavern Street in the mid 1950s, leaving behind a district where the first domestic gas burner had been lit and gas pipes laid as Ipswich started to embrace the new fuel that would eventually light most of the homes and streets before electricity was introduced. Allen Ransome, a wealthy industrialist, was the recipient of that initial gas light in his home in Carr street. Somewhat ostentatiously he lit a pound note with the flame, no doubt demonstrating that he had money to burn. Tavern Street had been lit by oil lamps since 1791, helping create a smoky atmosphere that Charles Dickens might have drawn upon when describing fogs in the capital city that he referred to as a 'London peculiar'. We had our own fogs and smogs even in the middle of the 20th century until successive Clean Air Acts helped create a healthier environment. There has been an inn on the corner of Tavern Street and Northgate Street since 1518, if not earlier. The Great White Horse Hotel can claim to have been patronised by George II, Louis XVIII and Horatio Nelson. It was rebuilt in the early 19th century and has, in more recent times, defied the developer's attempts to ruin one of the town's grandest landmarks.

Below: This part of town where St Matthew's Street met St George's Street, as viewed from Crown Street, is sometimes referred to as Hyde Park Corner. Most of the buildings, except for those on the far left, have long since disappeared as the road was widened and redesigned. On 18 January 1956, to the far right, Smith's Albion House was a popular store selling furniture and household goods. The cyclists were passing the Rainbow, a pub that once had a flourishing wines and spirits business. Many societies and organisations held functions in its rooms until closure came upon it in November 1961. The policeman on point duty was a familiar figure at busy junctions, a sight that is seldom seen today. Sometimes in a white coat and on other occasions just with white sleeves or a pair of gloves added to his uniform to mark him out, his carefully choreographed hand and arm movements could orchestrate the flow of traffic better than Sir Thomas Beecham could conduct the London Philharmonic. Nor did the British bobby require the frantic blowing of whistles that French and Italian police could not manage without. They worked themselves into a frenzy whilst our boy in blue, or white as the case might be, calmly made his directions clear to the motorists approaching the junction.

Right: The single decker bus trundling into the Cornhill has just passed under the archway that was created in 1931 when existing buildings were opened up to provide access to the newly built Lloyds Avenue. This elevated view of Westgate Street from Tavern Street looks along the route that was once part of the main road from the town to London. Mighty coaches were once driven along this thoroughfare, pulled by teams of horses, carrying both passengers and the mail to and from the capital. Several of the hotels and inns had large stables and coaching yards, but little evidence of these remains, although you can still see the original courtyard belonging to the Great White Horse Hotel further back on Tavern

Street. The building behind the double decker bus belonged to the tailoring business of John Henry Grimwade. He was described on one of his advertising leaflets as being 'a merchant tailor, woollen draper, hatter and hosier, specialist in juvenile suits and ready mades equal to bespoke'. In other words, it was a top notch outfit selling top notch outfits. Grimwade's, like so many other family businesses, could not compete with the changing fads of fashion and the cost cutting ploys of the large chain stores. Clinton Cards now occupy the premises. Perhaps this shop has an in memoriam card for the passing of Grimwade's.

All these houses were demolished in the 1960s as James Street fell victim to the demolition men swinging a ball from a crane that reduced to just so much rubble the bricks and mortar in which generations of families had lived. In their stead came the ill fated Greyfriars development whose shops lasted a fraction of the time that James Street had stood. The last time these people got together in such a way was at the end of the war when those same tables and benches, probably borrowed from a schoolroom or church hall, had been dragged out into the middle of the street. Perhaps some of the flags and bunting had been dusted off and pressed back into use, but the picture of the Queen was obviously brand new. She had come to the throne on 6 February 1952 when her father, George VI, had passed away. A heavy smoker, he had been ill for some time but had seemed sufficiently recovered for his daughter to tour the Commonwealth. She was in Kenya when his sudden deterioration threw a heavy burden on her young shoulders. By the time of the Coronation, nearly 16 months later, the country had recovered from its grief and pushed out the boat in celebrating the official recognition of Elizabeth II as our monarch. 'Vivat regina!' we all shouted, or words to that effect.

Left: Fore Hamlet's Gardener's Arms had obviously had a makeover as it looked so bright and shiny in the autumnal sunshine of 1 October 1948. Ipswich wanted to present a new face to the world in those immediate postwar years so this was a time when it continued the rehousing programme it had begun in the late 1920s and 1930s. Many of the older and insanitary properties had been swept away to be replaced by new estates that ringed the town. Gainsborough included street names of other famous painters and the Rivers estate had such watery roads as Severn, Medway and Trent. Greenwich estate took its name from a farm that once stood on the land, but most of the residents cared little for the origins as they were happy to be in homes with hot water, bathrooms and electricity. Even so, in 1948 there was still a major problem

with housing and reconstruction became a priority. All the while the Gardener's Arms sold its famous brew one that had been bubbling away since 1746 when the Cobbolds founded their brewery at Cliff Quay using water from Holywells. The family also had commercial interests in shipbuilding and banking. In the 19th century John Chevalier Cobbold was heavily involved in railway development and also served as a Member of Parliament, 1847-68. His son Felix also became an MP and provided the land for Fore Street Baths as well as presenting Christchurch Mansion to the town in 1896.

Above left: This scene is viewed from Upper Orwell Street looking into Fore Street, with Orwell Place to the right and Eagle Street to the left. The poles supporting the trolley bus wires were still in place in 1961 but they would become redundant two years later. This is one of the parts of the town that is still instantly recognisable today and even the build up of traffic at this crossroads has not altered one jot. We are fortunate in Ipswich that so much of our 20th century history remains intact and, whether young or old, we can relate to photographs such as this one. So many other towns in this country have been badly ripped apart by flyovers, new roads, concrete office blocks and shopping

malls that their hearts and souls seem to have been removed as well. There have been changes to the Ipswich skyline, but thankfully they are modest in comparison with many others. Except for the fashion styles of the pedestrians and the year of manufacture of the cars this could almost be a picture taken just the other day. The Spread Eagle, a pub that gave its name to Eagle street, formerly Rope Lane, looks very much the same. It is one of four inns that once stood at this junction and retained its olde worlde style even when it was rebuilt in 1850.

Top: 'He was a grand baker, me dad, and every morning he used to get me mam to push the freshly made loaves of Hovis up the hill in her pram so that she could make breakfast for us and the nine kids when we had nobbut two ha'pennies to rub together. First up was best dressed in those days and if we had two pieces of meat in the stew on our plates at teatime we used to shout snap'. Such exaggerations might make us chuckle, but life in the terraced housing on Great Whip Street was not a bed of roses in the 1950s. Even rationing did not completely disappear until 1954 as the difficult economic times of the immediate postwar period continued longer than most of us had thought possible. Many of the people living in the Stoke area were happy to have employment in the locomotive yards or at Ransome's, but it needed hard work to put down a pay packet each week that provided enough to guarantee a decent standard of living for the family. Housewives also had the toil of looking after the home without the aid of many of the modern electrical appliances. Carpets were beaten and washing done by hands reddened from hours spent at the kitchen sink and with the dolly tub and mangle. At least there was a decent baker's nearby to provide good bread for the sandwiches in hubby's lunchbox. Haward's stood on the corner of Felaw Street, named after the Tudor benefactor who left his house on Foundation Street to the grammar school. All these pictured houses have long been demolished and the A137 now separates Wherstead Road from this district.

The photographer stood outside the Great White Horse Hotel in 1961 looking from Tavern Street into Carr Street. Policing the crowd was an easy job as we had much better manners than are on display in modern times and bobbies were also treated with respect as custodians of the law with friendly faces. The atmosphere was relaxed, as can be seen from the body language of both police and spectators, and idle chitchat was happily exchanged without any question of rancour or aggression. The domed spire in the distance belonged to the premises of the East Anglia Daily Times. Its distinctive presence was lost to Carr Street in 1966 when it was demolished to make way for Carr Precinct, now Eastgate, shopping centre to be built. The Wimpy Bar on the corner with Northgate Street was one of the first of the fast food chains to make inroads into the nutritional requirements of the British stomach. Gradually the dietary picture changed and little cafés and small restaurants began to be squeezed out in favour of burger bars, big Macs and pizza palaces. The aroma of good old fish and chips, soaking in vinegar and encased in the soggy back page of the 'Evening Star', gave way to that of fried onions and cheese. By the end of the last century the transformation was complete when chicken tikka massala had become our national dish.

Above: Fore Street, as seen from Angel Lane in 1961, with the swimming pool to the left was home to Smyth Brothers, the well known ironmongers. Wells butcher's shop next door was particularly well known for the succulence of its pork sausages. Older readers mouths are probably watering already at the memory of those delicacies sizzling and spitting in the pan, giving off delicious aromas that just begged to be sniffed. How on earth can modern supermarkets try to pretend that their sawdust and bus ticket filled skins can be regarded as true British sausages? They are a poor, pale image of the true item. The Angel Street hoardings advertised a production of 'Random Harvest' at the Ipswich Theatre. This was a stage version of the 1941 James Hilton novel about a shell shocked officer in the 1914-18 war who is suffering from amnesia. It was made into a popular film in 1942, starring the top box office stars Ronald Colman and Greer Garson. In the 1930s Hilton wrote 'Goodbye Mr Chips' and 'Lost Horizon', both of which crossed over as big money spinners in the movies. The Lion and Lamb, a building that also used to be Alexander Christie's pawn shop, and the Angel pubs once stood on either side of this part of Angel Lane. The latter had stabling for 40 horses and once boasted its own brewery. Some of this area became a car park and was greatly altered as part of the new road development.

Below: The first signs of the change to the face of Ipswich town centre were just beginning to appear on 20 September 1963. The gable end of Walton's had started to receive the attention of the demolition men who would eventually knock down all this side of St Matthew's Street. Berners Street, alongside Stead and Simpson on the left, now opens onto the roundabout at the junction of St Matthew's Street and Civic Drive. The new buildings built here instead were erected behind the old building line, enabling the road to be widened. Walton's sold surgical appliances that included various types of stockings for those suffering from varicose veins. Women could have protruding parts of their anatomy squashed into a new shape by the corsets on offer, whilst trusses and special belts could be acquired by men wishing to gain something more than moral support. If all that makes your eyes water at the painful thought then perhaps the reader can make a mental visit to the shop next door and buy a quarter of barley sugars, stored in a large glass jar, to suck on the way home. Whilst in there buy a copy of Bunty for one of the children because this week there is a special pull out section that has a paper model of a girl on which cut out clothes can be hung. That should keep your daughters quiet, folding over the securing tabs on the model's frocks, as you settle down and watch TV to find out whether Minnie Caldwell's wayward pussycat, Bobby, has been found on 'Coronation Street'.

Left: The woman in front of the railings outside the supermarket, bags in hand, looks to be about to do battle with the lad pedalling towards her. Our money is on her in any confrontation, for she looks well set to swing a haymaker should the need arise. Even in 1961 schoolboys were expected to wear their schoolcaps, even if they had passed into that advanced stage of wearing long trousers. Prefects were posted near the school gates with the power to fine errant pupils threepence should they come into view improperly dressed. The money went into school funds, but some of the less responsible sixth formers made a profit on the side when they

declared that no one had fallen foul of them that day. The poor first former who had felt his ear tweaked and pocket money lightened was not about to split on someone six years older and considerably larger as retribution would have been even more painful. The mum crossing St Helen's Street had made sure that her children had little flags to wave when the Queen came past on her way to open the College. A royal visit was an important occasion and had to be marked properly. The Elmo in front of her was one of the first supermarkets in the town, heralding the start of the decline of the individual grocer and corner shop. It was built on the site of the old Beehive Inn that opened in 1899, but was one of the attractive buildings lost to Ipswich when it was pulled down in 1960.

Far left: When viewing the Fore Street-Salthouse Street junction today it is unlikely that you have time to draw breath as you negotiate the traffic filtering onto the road alongside Wherry Quay as it races off towards the A137 and its exit route to the A14. In 1961 just a solitary bicycle made its way past the hoarding that suggested smoking Player's cigarettes was a good way of improving your love life. Within a few years 'You're never alone with a Strand' and similar slogans would be removed from our television screens forever. Before the anti smoking lobby had its way there was even an

attempt to suggest that cigarettes were not only sexy but beneficial. In earlier times Craven A had been advertised with the message to smoke them 'for your throat's sake', but even in the 60s Consulate promoted its menthol flavoured coffin nails as 'cool as a mountain stream'. The chap on the stepladder was putting up decorations in anticipation of Queen Elizabeth's visit to open the Civic College. Behind him, Salthouse Street acted as a reminder of old trading days when the street ran down to Common Quay. The actual salt house, where the imported product was refined and stored, stood near the quay. In the 18th century salt was brought in by boat from the saltpans on the Tyne and from Nantwich, via the port at Liverpool.

At leisure

Above: The Chicken Run was one of the original wooden stands at Portman Road, but it was later dismantled and moved to Foxhall Stadium where it was a casualty of the 1987 gales. The annual primary schools athletics were dominated by running races rather than including the full range of track and field disciplines. After all, which schools for the under 11s could offer facilities for throwing the javelin or taking part in the pole vault? Some of these youngsters would have had difficulty in lifting a shot, never mind putting it. But that did not prevent the competitors from treating it all with the utmost seriousness for they raced to the tape with all the vigour of a Wilma Rudolph or Armin Hary, the gold medal winners from the Rome Olympics. Television was in most of our homes by then and children could model their performances on the stars they saw on the sports programmes beamed into our living rooms. How proud we were when a Briton performed nobly against all the odds. Peter Radford won a bronze medal in the 100m sprint in 1960, whilst Dorothy Hyman went one better, winning silver in the women's race. For young athletes who enjoyed watching longer races there was the sight of Middlesex's 'mighty mouse', the bespectacled Don Thompson. He prepared for the heat of an Italian summer by spending hours in a steam filled bathroom at home and was rewarded when his rolling gait carried him to the gold medal in the 50 kilometre walk.

ooking like an embryo Harry Potter in his 1960s glasses the little lad kneeling centre front cheered gustily in this posed picture at Portman Road. His mum had obviously advised him to make sure that he did not catch a chill, so he kept his jumper on just as he had been told. Presumably he was allowed to strip it off when he took part in one of the races that would be run as part of the primary schools athletics events that were regularly held at the soccer ground. Children's spectacles have undergone significant changes since these pupils were at school for now there are all sorts of designer frames and at designer prices, too. When these kiddies filed into class the short sighted from poorer families wore wire frames covered with pink plastic. The ones suffering from a squint had a blob of cotton padding taped over one lens and playground skirmishes usually led to the specs ending up twisted and lopsided, perched precariously upon a pair of ears rubbed red raw at the back. Parents wishing to kit out their offspring with something other than National Health monstrosities had a choice of round frames or Buddy Holly look alike ones as sported by the lad on the right. Note how the girls have been denied centre stage in the photograph, though one pretty Polly was doing her best to bellow for attention.

Speedway was one of the boom sports as things returned to normality after the second world war. Spectators, denied the regular opportunity of packing stadiums and sporting arenas, turned out in droves to stand on the terraces or sit in the stands and halls and wallow in the pleasure and excitement brought to them by professional athletes of one sort or another. Crowds queued at the turnstiles to watch the county cricket championship, a competition only watched by a handful these days. Soccer grounds had to turn away spectators who had not the sense to turn up an hour before the kick off and boxing matches were a sell out in theatres and halls over the country. All these sports had been popular before the war, but the four lap race around a cinder track was previously a minority sport. Not so in the late 1940s and 1950s as it became a boom enterprise. The Ipswich Witches roared around the Foxhall Stadium track from the early 50s, attracting a large following, though with mixed success. These riders made up the 1960 team that finished the season in a creditable fourth place. Jackie Unstead, one of the team's stars, was killed in a crash at Foxhall Stadium on 13 April 1962.

Standing (left to right) Vic Gooden promoter, Len Silver, Birger Forsberg, Peter Moore, Jack Unstead, Jimmy Squibb and Maurice Littlechild team manager.

Front row: Ray Cresp, Les McGillivray (team captain, on bike), and Jackie Biggs.

Left: Flat caps were still standard uniform for many football supporters even in the swinging 60s. Watching the game was also very much a male thing as the number of women in the crowd would struggle to exceed those on the pitch at halftime when the Dagenham Girl Pipers provided the entertainment. Portman Road was packed at the end of the 1961-62 season as Town celebrated the remarkable success of landing the First Division championship. The mascots of those days dressed up more sedately than the ones we see decorating the 21st century grounds. Some of the new ones that come visiting are quite amusing, including as they do Cyril the Swan from Swansea and Oldham's Ollie Owl, though Manchester United's Fred is a sad disappointment. However, 40 years or more ago club mascots did not compete with one another in their dress, nor did they fight as some have been known to do in recent times. They were happy just to proclaim their allegiance to their hometown club, something difficult for supporters of modern football to claim as they support teams that play hundreds of miles distant from their birthplace. Miss Switch was very much a local girl, though she probably owed some of the inspiration for her title to the speedway club. The old chap standing next to her was a regular at Portman Road. This cheerleader boasted the nickname 'Swede' and could be seen as a bus conductor in real life.

Below: EH Bostock was one of the town's leading entertainment entrepreneurs in the early 20th century. He founded the Hippodrome in 1905 and also added the Lyceum Theatre and cinema to his empire in 1920. The Hippodrome hosted music hall acts, variety shows and pantomimes in its early days. Those were great days for entertainers who could tour the country with an act that required no addition to its content as they went from theatre to theatre. A booking at the Bolton Grand could follow a stint at the Ipswich Hippodrome and then it was off to the Glasgow Empire. There was little chance of any member of the Suffolk audience being present in Lancashire or Scotland to witness the same jokes, songs or dance routines being repeated. A performer could hone material to perfection whilst on the road, knowing that revision would only be required when a return visit was made some time later. It was television that caused the break up of the variety scene, for once millions had seen a performance on the small screen there was no chance of repeating it onstage without incurring the wrath of a disgruntled audience. The Hippodrome started showing films in the 1930s in response to the clamour for the newfangled talkies from Hollywood. By 1941 it had become a revue theatre and, on 14 April 1955, was advertising acts that were 'red hot from Paris' for 'Ooh! What a night', doubtless a show not designed for your maiden aunt to enjoy.

The Hippodrome became the Savoy ballroom in 1957 at a time when dancing cheek to cheek was still in vogue. Youngsters were sent off to Saturday morning classes to learn the intricacies of spin turns, palais glides, fishtails and chassis steps so that they could perform confidently on the dance floor at Aunt Bessie's wedding reception and on Saturday nights at the Savoy. Ballroom dancing was one of the social graces that we all mastered from whatever walk of life we came. Live bands played standards and popular hit tunes of the day. The girls sat at tables around the edge of the floor, giggling together as some pimply youth came over with the well practised chat up line of 'Are you dancing?' hoping to be answered with 'I'm dancing'. When lads came over in pairs how was it that your mate always seemed to pull the goodlooking one and you were left with his awkward pal? Still, that was better than sitting it out as a wallflower, wishing the floor would open just to swallow you up. As the 60s went by dance halls began to fall out of favour, being replaced by smaller clubs in cellars where four piece groups belted out American influenced beat music. At the Savoy there was still a balance of the old and the new, even on 29 February 1964. Cilla Black was top of the pops with 'Anyone who had a heart', a song to smooch to if ever there was one. Inevitably the Savoy became a bingo hall and was demolished in 1985.

Events & occasions

The Duke of Sussex in Cumberland Street was festooned with balloons and bunting, flags and fancy decorations as the locals waited to celebrate the 1937 Coronation. Politically, it was an anxious era at home and abroad. The Spaniards were waging a war amongst themselves in which the little Basque town of Guernica was almost wiped off the map by German bombers that had joined in to help Franco's fascist forces. It was an evil portent of the blitz upon our own country three years later. In 1936 our monarchy had suffered a crisis when, following the death of George V, Edward VIII became king. His dalliance with the American socialite Wallis Simpson exploded into a

major controversy that rocked the church and government. She was twice divorced and no fit partner for the head of the Commonwealth and the Church of England in the moral and social climate of that time. Pressure from the establishment caused him to abdicate before Christmas and his brother, the Duke of York, took over the mantle of monarchy. He was crowned amidst great excitement on 12 May 1937, the very day originally set aside for his brother's coronation. Every town and village in the land celebrated the occasion with processions, parades and carnivals. Three weeks later the former king married Mrs Simpson in a French chateau and we consigned his brief reign to the history books.

Below: Taken from the roof of Egerton's motor showrooms and repair centre the crowds in front of Tower Ramparts School had gathered to listen to the speeches and proclamations about to be made on VE Day when we celebrated the conclusion of hostilities in Europe. Peace came on 7 May 1945 when the Allied Supreme Commander, General Eisenhower, accepted the German surrender. The following day the news was announced in Britain and all the drabness and privation of the previous six years were forgotten in a blaze of fireworks, floodlights and coloured flags. In Whitehall 'good old Winnie' was cheered to the heavens when he appeared on the Ministry of Health balcony. However, we Brits are a fickle breed because we voted Churchill out of office just over two months later in the general election. VE Day celebrations in Ipswich were just as noisy and joyous as the rest of the country, but tempered with sadness for those who were destined to a future without a loved one left on some foreign field. The gathering took place in front of the former Municipal Secondary School for Boys that opened in 1906, but was demolished in the 1970s. The site is now used by the shopping centre that opened here on 7 November 1986.

Above: Brookfield Road is just off Norwich Road, close to the railway line, but it could have been anywhere in England in May 1945. Nearly every street looked exactly the same, festooned with bunting that had been stored away since the 1937 coronation and containing dozens of smiling faces all ready to enjoy a street party, the like of which they had never seen before. Mums rolled up their sleeves and did battle with the meagre resources they had in order to put on a spread that the children would remember for the rest of their lives. A gramophone was wound up and someone found an old needle that had not been sacrificed as part of the war effort when any spare scrap of metal had been contributed to go towards the manufacture of another Hurricane, tank or destroyer. A neighbour donated a treasured copy of 'We'll meet again' and it was played over and over, bringing tears to the eyes of those who knew someone with whom they would not be having a reunion until they passed over to the other side. In truth, that was every single one of those who had collected together to celebrate, but also to give thanks for their deliverance. The adults put on a brave face for the sake of the children and replaced the record on the turntable with 'Mairzy Doats' so that they could play musical chairs and laugh again.

Grange Road, not far from Alexandra Park, was one of thousands of streets up and down the country that threw parties to celebrate the end of the war in Europe. Bunting was stretched across the street and flags fluttered gaily in the breeze. All the residents posed before moving off to the tables in the middle of the road at which they could tuck into the food provided by blowing jealously guarded and carefully hoarded ration coupons for one big bash. The children scoffed most of the grub for there was not that much to go round and, after all, this war had been fought to ensure their future in a free world. The little ones at the front of the group, in their jolly party hats, had known nothing but wartime deprivation. To them the world must have seemed one of iron rations and falling bombs. What a harsh place it must have seemed. It was one that took away their fathers and elder brothers, some permanently. Look among the crowd of people on Grange Road that day and see how many young men you can spot. Britain had become a land of women, middle aged men and grandfathers. When those serving in the forces returned to civvy street they had to forge relationships with children they hardly knew and pick up the threads again with wives and sweethearts who had waited patiently for so long.

Above: Someone with an eye for symmetry must have arranged this picture as it almost looks as if two photos have been fused together to create this effect of the gathering on Lancing Avenue, just off Colchester Road. Street parties were not frequent occurrences during the 20th century, but they took place when there were moments of national celebration. Some rejoicing took place when Edward VII, George V and George VI were crowned, as it did when the armistice was signed to end World War I. But it was with the end of the second world war that the community really got together to put on a show that would send a message to the rest of the world that we had fought together and now we were going to party together. A similarly euphoric mood hit the country in 1953 when Elizabeth II was crowned. Just as eight years earlier,

and friends began to move away and become more mobile, the spirit was revived for the silver jubilee in 1977. The 2002 golden jubilee festivity preparations had more difficulties to cope with when the nanny state insisted on licences and application forms being completed just to hold a street party.

Top: The Fifty Shilling Tailor, on the corner of Upper Brook Street, was the brainchild of Henry Price. Acknowledging that, despite money being tight during the years leading up to the war, men still wanted to dress as elegantly as they could afford. He spotted a niche in the market and established his tailor's, selling cheap, but acceptable, clothing. Soon he had a chain of stores across the country that remained popular throughout the 1950s until greater prosperity and a desire for more fashionable clothing altered purchasing patterns. Price died in 2000, but left a legacy of fond memories of the days when a man's suit cost just £2.50, in today's terminology. The procession wending its way from Carr Street into Tavern Street was part of the Coronation celebrations of 2 June 1953, a dank and dismal day in terms of the weather, but a bright and cheerful one in our hearts as we raised our hats to the Queen who was being officially invested in Westminster Abbey, just over a year after acceding to the throne on the death of George VI. The parade wended its way past Croydon's, the jeweller who can trace a family history through seven generations buying wedding rings since 1865. 'Happiness starts with a Croydon engagement ring' and the slogan is not referring to that concrete jungle in Greater London.

out came the trestle tables, flags and bunting because we saw the coronation of a young monarch as being the start of a new era when we could leave the old one, full of death and despair, far behind. In those now far off days our parents and grandparents lived in their neighbours' pockets and there was a true community spirit easy to tap into when organising a street party. Everyone naturally chipped in. Surprisingly, as families

Above: Daft hats, bright decorations and a sense of fun were some of the ingredients brought to Beck Street by the Coronation in 1953. It might have been a bit chilly for June, but the British have never been a people to let a little matter like the weather spoil the party. Just look at us when we go on holiday. We get down to the beach at our allotted time and sit there oblivious to the howling gale or gathering storm clouds that have driven Johnny foreigner off the sands. Alternatively, we bare our pale torsos under a scorching sun whilst enjoying the process of turning into a painful lobster. Mad dogs and Englishmen is about right. There was little chance of sunstroke on Beck Street, but the threat of rain did not dampen the appetites of these children. What wonderful manners they had, waiting patiently as the photographer snapped away while they were sorely tempted by the array of fairy cakes, potted meat sandwiches, biscuits and orangeade just begging to be devoured. Their good behaviour took a bit of a battering when the word was given to attack the spread in front of them. A mountain of jellies, made in moulds shaped like rabbits and pussycats, disappeared in a flash. What had taken the mums hours to prepare disappeared in a matter of minutes. Where did those little monkeys put it all?

Ridley & Son was a gents' clothier more upmarket than most and if your suit was bought from this tailor's then you were worth a bob or two. That mattered for nothing on 2 June 1953, for we were all equal subjects of Queen Elizabeth II who was being crowned that day in Westminster Abbey. Marching bands and gaily decorated floats made their way through town past cheering crowds enjoying the pageantry of the occasion. Back home one family carefully drew the curtains shut and switched on its new toy. After what seemed a lifetime a flickering black and white picture appeared on the screen of the little box in the corner. Images of the royal procession and the gold coach making its way through the London streets at walking pace came into the living room. Within minutes this family had acquired a set of friends it never knew it had as neighbours crowded in through the door to share the experience and listen to the sonorous tones of the commentator, Richard Dimbleby. The mood was lightened by the sight of Queen Salote of Tonga, a huge and beaming figure who waved vigorously to the crowds as her open carriage filled with rainwater. After Queen Elizabeth and Prince Philip had appeared on the balcony of Buckingham Palace for the umpteenth time the television was turned off. The viewers watched the white spot on the screen gradually disappear and then went out into the street for a party that went on until dusk.

Below left: The nurse hoped that her skills would not be required to treat any fainting fits amongst the crowd of people crushed tightly together waiting for Her Majesty to drive past. There was every danger of that happening because it was a bright and sunny day. If anyone keeled over she would have administered first aid, but would have been mortified to do so if the moment coincided with the royal visitor's arrival. The waiting went on for hours and there would only be a few seconds when the head of the Commonwealth would be in full view. The scene was captured behind the Town Hall outside the Westminster Bank at the junction where Princes Street, Kings Street, Queens Street and Butter Market all meet. There are a number of banks and finance houses close to this part of town, tracing their ancestry to the end of the 18th century when we had two banks. Alexander's, that became Gurney's in 1878, was also known as the Yellow Bank because of its partners' support for the Whig party. Business in the Ipswich Town and Country Bank, founded in 1786 by Crickitt, Truelove and Kerridge, was later continued by Bacon, Cobbold and Co. As they were adherents to the Tory party theirs became the Blue Bank. Alexander's dealings provided the opportunity for an early version of the 1963 Great Train Robbery when the London to Ipswich horse drawn mail coach was robbed of £31,199, a fabulous sum two centuries ago.

Bottom: All manner of groups and organisations gathered on the football pitch ready to greet the Queen as her car drove into the stadium. North Stand, to the left, and the Chicken Run, to the right, were packed with spectators anxious to grab a glimpse of the monarch who was driven around the ground in an open topped car. On 21 July 1961, as the military band, scout groups, display teams etc awaited her arrival, British troops had landed in Kuwait in anticipation of an attack by Iraq. Some things never change, for 30 years later we would again be involved in helping this little state against its predatory neighbour in the Gulf War. In 1961 things were just as ominous as a nervous world feared that minor conflicts could escalate into global strife. The Russian premier Khruschev muttered dark threats about our involvement in a year that had already seen the Bay of Pigs fiasco, when American troops entered Cuba, and would later see the erection of the Berlin Wall. The visit of the Queen to Portman Road provided a pleasant respite from international troubles. Since the day when she graced the football ground with her presence the Chicken Run was moved to the speedway stadium and, in 2002, a modern one was replacing the old North Stand.

Above: How many of these little loves spilling over in front of the barriers on the Cornhill had been dressed by Footman's, the department store that proclaimed itself to be East Anglia's top store? Standing underneath the union flags fluttering in the breeze, they had been given a lift over the crush rails so that they could get a better view of the Queen as her car hove into sight in front of the Town Hall in the summer of 1961. It was a good time to remind ourselves of the stability that the monarchy gave to Britain as the world outside was a dangerous place. Ever since the major powers had been stockpiling nuclear weapons nations faced each other with a suspicious air, ever wondering whose finger would be on the button to start World War III. Surely man would not be so mad as to plunge the globe into another conflict that could be the end of us all this time? The pessimists reminded those who wanted to listen that we had ignored the horrors of the Great War and embarked on another only 21 years later. The optimists put their trust in God and grabbed what solace they could from waving their flags in support of a monarchy that had, since the civil war of the 17th century, outlasted all attempts to bring it down.

Below: Little children skipped onto the road of Fore Street as they waited for the Queen to pass by in the summer of 1961. They had their little flags clutched tightly in their hands, ready to wave them the very moment that the royal car came into sight. Modern mums in the crowd wore the very latest in fashionable frocks with floral patterns and billowing skirts over freshly starched petticoats that stopped below the knee. By the end of the decade those hemlines would be more like pelmets as Mary Quant and her fellow designers pushed them ever higher, much to the delight of all redblooded males and the disgust of their fathers. It was always amusing to watch your own dad sneak a look at a long legged Jean Shrimpton type and then mutter something about what the world was coming to. But in 1961 bare arms were about as risqué as we could dare to be, for they were still the days when churchgoing women always wore a hat to attend Sunday service. Hair that was worn fairly short would also be subjected to a fashion revolt that arrived even before the mini skirt. Large tresses were backcombed into a beehive shape and stayed towering above our heads thanks to liberal doses of lacquer sprayed over the creation. Dad gave up on us completely.

Above: The huge number of women and children in the crowd at Portman Road gives the game away that this 1961 scene is nothing to do with muddy oafs kicking a lump of leather around. On closer inspection the patriotic flags that some are holding gives us the final clue. The spectators are gathered to celebrate the Queen's visit, as shortly she will be driven onto the pitch to be greeted with affectionate cheers and loud applause. How dated those children's haircuts now look, especially those of the little boys. Short back and sides was the order of the day, with pudding basin shapes to the finished articles. By the end of the decade it would be all change as their ears disappeared underneath flowing locks that made the older generation mutter about effeminate fashion and bringing back national service to make men of them. These boys will now be about 50 and can still recall wearing jackets and ties when they went out with their parents, only to throw them away as they reached adulthood in favour of T-shirts and jeans. It was not the done thing to insult our monarch to be so casually attired over 40 years ago, so the Churchman Stand was filled with neatly turned out children. The stand took its name from William Churchman who founded his wholesale tobacco business in the late 18th century. The firm expanded into a new factory at the junction of Princes Street and Portman Road in 1898. From there it produced cigarette packets that contained collectable picture cards. Some of Churchman's earliest ones depicted East Anglian subjects.

Top right: The Queen has never been a football fan, though she has been guest of honour at most FA Cup Finals since the Blackpool-Bolton 1953 epic, the famous Matthews final. However, on this occasion Portman Road was merely being used as a large gathering place where her subjects could get together and acknowledge her visit to the town as part of the ceremonies connected with the opening of the new college. Happy snappers amongst the children captured the moment she was presented to local dignitaries before ascending the dais to speak to the thousands packed into the stands that a few weeks before had roared the Blues to a thumping 4-0 victory over Sunderland that ensured promotion to Division One for the first time in the club's history. But, on this day the reception the Queen received was more muted, if just as loyal. The Windsors were still regarded with great affection and many of us felt that we could relate to her, despite the regal manner and clipped speech. Strip away the privileges and she was a parent, just like the rest of us, a proud mother of three at the time. Her youngest, Andrew, was just a toddler and Elizabeth was still a young woman and mum, whatever other baggage she carried.

Far right: Queen Elizabeth II, as gracefully as ever, pulled the cord that released the covers over the plaque on the wall at the new Civic College. She was dressed in a co-ordinated fashion as she always was on such occasions and her hosts put on their ceremonial robes, chains of office and university gowns in honour of the special day and their important guest. The first students to enrol would have

been war babies, closely followed by those born in the baby boomer years of the late 1940s. Many of that first cohort will now be looking forward to the end of their days in the workplace, if they have not already taken early retirement. No such luck for Her Majesty who, on 21 July 1961, still had over 40 years' more service to give, and still counting. In more recent times many colleges and polytechnics have been upgraded to university status. Now renamed Suffolk College, in 1992 it became an accredited part of the University of East Anglia providing a wide range of subjects and modes of study. The College enrols approximately 4,800 full-time, 8,400 part-time and 12,000 adult, leisure and recreational course students annually. Those students on programmes of study that lead to formal qualifications are split between higher and further education courses.

They climbed lampposts, swung off awnings and perched on every ledge and balcony possible to get the best view of the team that conquered Europe. Anyone dropping from the top of Burton's would have to hope that he fell into a new suit. Even a pair of bobbies got a good vantage point, ostensibly in the interests of watching over the crowd for safety reasons, but they cheered as loudly as anyone else when Bobby Robson's team came into sight on the Cornhill. On 24 May 1981 the UEFA Cup came to Ipswich. Until 1971 this competition was known as the Fairs Cup and, under either name, had been won by a number of English sides, including Leeds, Spurs, Newcastle, Liverpool and Arsenal. In 1981 it was time for Ipswich to join that exalted crew. Robson was a shrewd manager, one of the first to spot the potential of introducing foreigners from whom home grown players could learn a thing or two. He brought the Dutchmen Arnold Muhren and Frans Thijssen to Portman Road, installing them into midfield roles where they could control the play. The final was played over two legs and it seemed as if the tie was all over when opponents AZ '67 were easily beaten 3-0. The return in Amsterdam caused many heart stopping moments as Town went down 2-4 for the narrowest of aggregate wins. Bobby Robson went on to manage England and came within a whisker of emulating Alf Ramsey, but his national side lost the penalty shoot out to Germany in the 1990 World Cup semi final.

Above: Our beloved monarch came to the throne in the winter of 1952 and in the early summer of 1977 she went on a tour of her realm in anticipation of the celebrations for her silver jubilee. The sun shone brightly on her the day she came to Ipswich. Loyal subjects pressed little posies into her hand and waved their flags under her nose. This was a more accessible queen than the one we had seen in the earlier days of her reign when she was usually tucked away behind the glass windows of her limousine.

The younger generation that was supposed to view the monarchy with some indifference gave the lie to that statement as can be seen from the happy smiles that greeted her walkabout on Cornhill with Mayor David Myer. At the start of the year talk of the jubilee celebrations was all gloom and doom. There seemed to be little interest in pushing the boat out. The royal family was undergoing some hiccoughs in its public relations department. Princess Margaret's marriage was on the rocks and

Top: The Duke of Edinburgh, then a comparatively young man of 31, landed at a snowy Martlesham Heath in 1953 to be greeted by Lord lieutenant Earl Stradbroke. The aerodrome was established during World War I and, in the 1920s, developed as an experimental testing station. During World War II it was used as a fighter base by the RAF and American air forces, but is most fondly remembered for its association with Douglas Bader, the remarkable pilot who lost his legs in an aerial accident in the early 1930s. Despite his handicap he returned to the skies and commanded 242 Squadron at Martlesham and it was no surprise to those who knew him that he stoically endured imprisonment as a POW when shot down on active service. When Prince Philip landed at the aerodrome he was on a peaceful mission, but one that had already claimed many lives. Violent storms had been lashing much of Britain early in the year. Mountainous seas off Stranraer hit the Irish Sea car ferry Princess Victoria and 128 lost their lives when water smashed in through cargo doors that had not been closed properly. On England's east coast hurricane force winds brought disaster as sea defences collapsed from Lincolnshire to north Kent. Canvey Island was devastated, Clacton was under water and many lives were lost in Norfolk as the death roll in East Anglia rose to 280. The Duke of Edinburgh offered moral support, but little could be done to ease the pain and suffering of so many.

she was featuring in the gossip columns when spotted holidaying with her 'friend' Roddy Llewellyn. In Parliament Willie Hamilton MP banged on about the waste of public money and the honouring of the 25 year reign looked like being a damp squib. How wrong the prophets of doom were. When 7 June arrived a week of festivities began, the like of which had not been seen for years as street parties were held and a carnival atmosphere swept the country.

Bird's eye view

The 1950s view of part of the town centre, looking north across towards Christchurch Park from what is now Cardinal Park, the site of modern night clubs and cinemas, has Portman Road and the edge of the football ground to the left. Over towards the bottom right a careful examination will pick out the tower of St Peter's near Stoke Bridge, probably the spot where Ipswich's first church was built in Anglo Saxon times as the town grew along the north bank of the Orwell in those days. Between the 12th century and the time when Henry VIII began his sweeping away of the monasteries, the Priory of St Peter and St Paul, built by the Augustinians, occupied the land above St Peter's. Cardinal Wolsey, after whom several local landmarks are named, was Henry VIII's Lord Chancellor. This son of an Ipswich butcher eventually fell out with the king, but not before he had exerted some major influence on the country's judicial institutions. He was also responsible for the building of the College of St Mary for which St Peter's was the chapel. Little remains of the college now, except for the south gate that stands to the east of the church. Wolsey was accused of treason in 1530, but died before he could be tried, possibly saving himself a more painful demise.

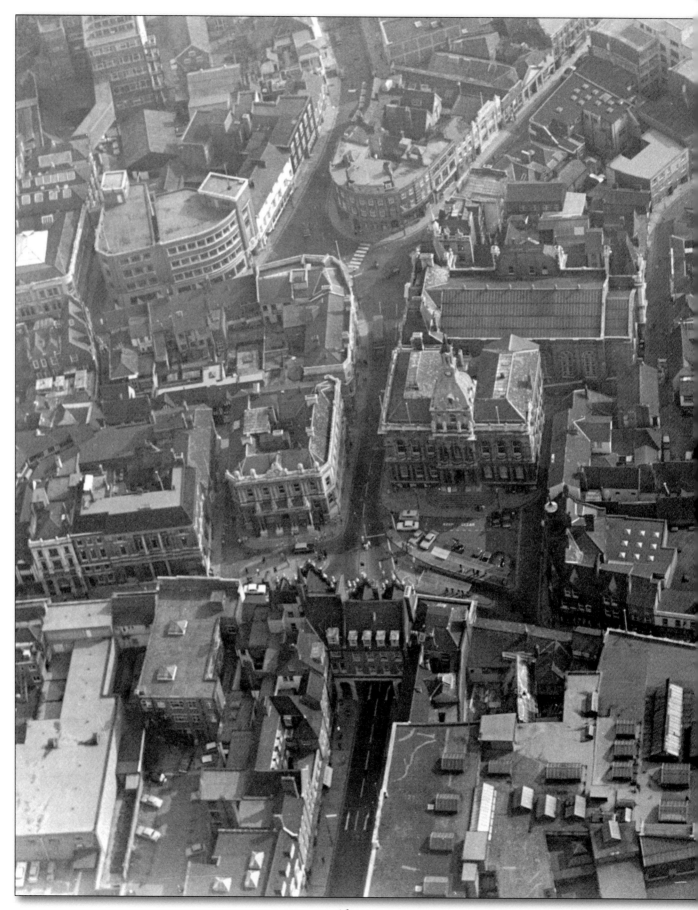

Left: This aerial view was taken c1970 and shows the main shopping areas of central Ipswich. Footman's, now Debenhams, is at the bottom centre as we look across the arcade straddling Lloyd's Avenue to Queen Street and Princes Street beyond. This famous department store was a family business, founded in 1815. John Footman was also one of those involved with the development of the Eastern Union Railway in 1846. Most towns have had a similar store in their histories, from Harvey's in Guildford to Binns in Sunderland. In nearly every case the giant chains have gradually swallowed them up, but some older residents still refer to them by their original names, not wanting to break with tradition. The Butter Market shopping centre now dominates the top left of this part of town, part of the redevelopment exercise begun over 20 years ago. The very centre of the picture is devoted to the Town Hall and Corn Exchange buildings. The former cost £16,000 to build in 1868 and, below its 120 foot clock tower, stand the four female figures that represent agriculture, learning, commerce and justice. To the left of the Town Hall stands the old Post Office, a fine edifice erected in 1882 of white Portland stone and Suffolk brick. Nearby, cars were parked along what is now a pedestrianised area all the way from Major's Corner to the Wolsey Theatre.

Above: Princes Street, as it looked in the 1950s, had been photographed from a position above the archway leading into Lloyds Avenue. In the distance the bus was turning into Queen Street at the junction with Butter Market and King Street. Across Princes Street from the Town Hall, the building on the left is now home to Lloyds TSB, but was originally the Post Office that was completed in 1882. It seems to have been a chilly day if the little figures hurrying and scurrying across the road are any evidence. They look to be well wrapped up and some are hunched against what might have been a chilly breeze. In the winter the high buildings along the town centre streets block out the sun for a large part of the day, casting them in shadow and making it feel colder than it really is. When these shoppers and office workers got home they could have mixed themselves a warming cup of Horlick's or a steaming mug of Oxo to get the chill out of their bones. This was not a time when the central heating was set to come on an hour before we got home as we relied on a bar on the electric fire or the hiss of the gas flame over which to warm our hands. But these were emergency and expensive forms of heat, so we raked the ashes out of the grate, screwed sheets of newspaper and set the coal ready for lighting. It took an age for the heat to come through, but it looked lovely when it got going.

Above: The back of the Butter Market shopping centre would now occupy part of the left hand side of this photograph, but on 12 October 1959 shoppers still went for their weekly order to the grocer, the butcher, the baker, the greengrocer and the dairy, all housed in separate outlets rather than under one roof. Supermarket was still a new word in our vocabulary and, in any case, we enjoyed the homely and cosy ambience of going to shops where we were greeted like old friends. But change was on the way as we moved into a period of greater prosperity, having put the austerity of the postwar years firmly behind us. Just three days earlier the country had returned Supermac, Harold Macmillan, to 10 Downing Street with a majority of 100 on the back of his slogan, 'You've never had it so good'. Passengers at the Eastern Counties bus depot in the Old Cattle Market, just beyond the Blue Coat Boy, agreed. Next to the depot is the Plough, a Cobbold house. Dog's Head Street, leading into Falcon Street, was once an even more congested area than in latter years, its narrow lane being fronted by houses just 15 feet apart across from each other in places. The Plough lost some of its own frontage when this road was widened. The building to the left of the photograph was the post office sorting house.

In May 1956 the photographer was perched high up on St Peter's Church in order to take this shot of St Peter's Street as it heads off towards St Nicholas Street. Just before the roadway reaches that point there is an attractive timber framed building on the corner of Silent Street. There is a plaque here to the memory of Thomas Wolsey, the Cardinal and statesman who dominated Henry VIII's government for 15 years. An inscription states that he died 'a humble man', but the truth is that he was highly unpopular and helped spark the anti clerical reaction that was a factor in the Reformation. Silent Street was widened in 1812 to assist the sale of cattle and horses in the old cattle market at the end of Silent Street, which must have been anything but given the amount of neighing and lowing that would have been taking place. It fell quiet in 1856 when the market was moved to a site near Portman Road. In 1956 one of the few threats to British car manufacturers from elsewhere in Europe can be seen on St Peter's Street. The rear engined Volkswagen was gaining in popularity, eventually inspiring Alec Issigonis to design the BMC Mini as a rival. Even so, the 'Beetle' still maintained a strong place in the market, having gained many friends since the 'people's car' was launched in 1937.

This glorious 1966 view across the river and port shows one of the reasons for Ipswich's rise to a position of national importance in days gone by. The Vikings also used the river as a means of access for their raiding parties, but we prefer to remember that it was from here that traders of the Middle Ages helped put the town on the commercial map. Activity stagnated in the 18th century when the Orwell silted up, but improvements to the channel and the building of the Wet Dock in 1842 rejuvenated Ipswich's fortunes. In this photograph, taken when the cheers of soccer fans were still ringing out in praise of Alf Ramsey's World Cup winning team, the cranes of Ransome and Rapier's engineering works can be seen at the Waterside Works on the left. Near here are the remains of the open air Stoke Bathing Place. Across the other side of the river, Cliff Quay is to the right with, above it, the gasholders of the old works and the Orwell works of Ransome, Sims and Jefferies. In the distance are the warehouses and quays along the Wet Dock where coal, grain and animal feed was stored and such as R & W Paul carried out their malting business. When the old Custom House on Common Quay, designed by JM Clark, was opened in 1845 it looked out on the largest area of enclosed water of its type in England.

The Civic Centre was under construction in the 1960s as the changing face of the town took shape. The new Civic Drive and Franciscan Way thoroughfare had little traffic on it, but was soon to collect more than its fair share of vehicles before too many years went by. Above the Civic Centre, with its collection of council offices, law courts and police station, Museum Street and Elm Street meet at the offset crossroads from where Museum Street leads towards where you will now find the curving black glass of the Willis building. Its use as an international insurance centre has been a modern feature of the town since 1975. Designed by Sir Norman Foster, unusually for such a recent building, it has been given Grade I listed status. Whilst it is not to everyone's taste there is no denying its striking appearance. Museum Street, to the left of the aerial view, was where one of Britain's first municipal museums was built in 1847, though it has now been rehoused on High Street. On the far side of the junction with Elm Street are Mrs Ann Smyth's almshouses, across from the attractively named church St Mary of the Elms where Huguenot weavers, refugees from religious persecution in mainland Europe, worshipped in the late 17th century. The Tudor brick tower stands above a much older doorway that goes back to the days of the Normans.

Above: Anyone suffering from vertigo should look away quickly. Such is the effect upon those of us with queasy tummies that looking straight down onto the ground below is enough to bring on an attack of the goosebumps. The scene underneath the aircraft from which this 1964 photograph was taken reminds us of an amphitheatre. Any moment now Russell Crowe might be walking out into the arena, armed with a sword and small shield, to salute Caesar before leaping into action. In reality the skirmishing taking place was conducted by earth movers, piledrivers and pneumatic hammers. The spiral car park taking shape is one of those oddities of 60s design. Unlike most of the monstrous and rectangular constructions of that decade, it was built with consideration for the environment and largely hidden from view underneath the ground. Alongside it, the creation of Civic Drive was under way around the time when a scheme was being floated to force expansion upon the town that would increase the population to somewhere in the region of 200,000. The effect would have been to produce the sort of concrete jungle and mixture of housing estates and high rise flats that have blighted so many of our towns as planners strove to satisfy the need of the false god they called progress. Happily for Ipswich the plan was dropped and today's population is just over half of what might have been foisted upon it.

Wartime

There is something sadly ironic that this wartime scene should show the bomb damage done to Cemetery Road and the memorial mason's premises on 21 September 1940. Ipswich had felt the first effect of aerial bombardment in Dale Hall Lane on 21 June when three people lost their lives, but the raids in the early autumn were much more destructive. London bore the brunt of the onslaught in what was to become an almost nightly occurrence until the beginning of the following summer, still referred to as 'the blitz'. Other towns and cities had their share of terror raining down upon them and this destructive strike was caused by a parachute mine. Over 150 houses were badly damaged and almost 2,000 were affected in some way during the attack, but more was to come from this particular bomb. It had not fully detonated and the royal Navy disposal team was called in to deal with it. As it was too volatile to be defused or moved the mine had to be detonated where it lay. Residents were evacuated and, two days later, a mighty explosion was caused that took out another 75 houses and damaged hundreds more. Air strikes continued on and off until 1943, but the lull was ended when, in the summer of 1944, flying bombs, followed by V-2 rockets, started to buzz in the skies overhead. They caused havoc in the capital and across Kent, but only two landed in Ipswich.

Above: The chap in the middle is not some form of 1940s Tractor Boy, waving his rattle to encourage the Blues on to more glory. He was Charlie Girling, a celebrated local photographer who had posed this picture with members of the civil defence Air Raid Precautions (ARP) personnel. They were taking cover during one of the wartime bombing runs that the Luftwaffe made on our towns, cities and industries as it attempted to damage our resources and shatter our resolve. Some success was achieved on the first, but not on the latter. Charlie's rattle was not put to any sporting use, but as a rather idiosyncratic form of early warning system that an air raid was on the way and it was time to take cover. Thankfully, we also had sirens that could alert people on a wider scale. Unfortunately, Charlie's photograph now conjures up pictures akin to the TV programme, 'Dad's Army', that suggest our defences at home were in the hands of silly people armed with broomsticks pretending to be of some importance, but really figures of fun. The truth was a long way from that impression because, after a haphazard beginning, dedicated, brave and professional groups of people in the ARP, Home Guard, Women's Voluntary Service, St John Ambulance and emergency services became what Churchill called 'the army that Hitler forgot'. The photograph was taken at WS Cowells, a town centre printing company.

On VE Day the inhabitants of James Street were ready for their party now that the war in Europe had come to an end. Hardly any of the young men who had gone off to fight had returned and the organisation of the celebrations was left to the women, children and old people who lived here. As they had their jam sandwiches and buns minds drifted off to thoughts of loved ones overseas. Some were on their way home, but others were still fighting their way through the jungles of the Far East for it would be another four months before the bombs dropped on Hiroshima and Nagasaki brought Japan to its knees. Then there were those who would never make it back, having paid the ultimate price for their defence of the realm. How many of these children would grow up never really having known their father? The widows remembered to their dying day the sense of dread when they heard that knock on the door and the postman delivered the telegram that they all feared. Even for those who were reunited with their husbands and sweethearts life was never quite the same again. They had lost vital years of learning about one another or seeing together their children growing up. Those were lost experiences that could never be reclaimed.

Below: They dragged out the tables into the middle of Waterworks Street to celebrate the announcement that six long years of conflict had come to an end. Union flags hung triumphantly above their heads as they tucked into carrot jam sandwiches and fairy cakes baked with egg substitute. These terraced houses, packed tightly together, represented the type of closely knit community that, like those very same homes, has disappeared into history as the residents moved away into newer council housing in the postwar era. VE Day represented the start of a new way of life with the break up of the old togetherness where you could pop

next door for a cup of sugar without bothering to lock the front door. Waterworks Street had been home to the old Ipswich fire engine station where the first manually operated pumps were housed. As well as owing its name to the works that were here helping to provide better sanitation against the killer typhoid, the street was also renowned for its infants' school. It became one of the new School Board establishments in 1872, having been one of the Ragged Schools formed to educate poor and needy children as the Victorians developed a social conscience. However, in May 1945 these children were merely needy of a good time and their mums made sure that is just what they got.

Bottom: A huge aircraft propeller was a novel table decoration for the residents of Gatacre Road, near Yarmouth Road, as they prepared to celebrate VE Day. Yet, it was probably very apt, for did we not have so much thanks to give to those who took to the skies and their back up teams on the ground? Without their bravery and technical skill there is every chance that we might have become another satellite of the 1,000 year Reich. In the years leading up to the war aircraft designers like Reginald Mitchell, the man behind the Spitfire, laid the basis for our air supremacy, but it took the heroism of young pilots to keep us safe when they beat off the enemy in the Battle of Britain during the late summer of 1940. 'Never in the field of human conflict was so much owed by so many to so few.' Later developments by Frank Whittle brought us the jet engine and there was the bouncing bomb invented by Barnes-Wallis used with great effect by Guy Gibson's Dambusters on the Mohne and Eder dams. The families enjoying these celebrations had raided the school at the end of the street for trestles and stools. Even though belts had to be tightened for the next few days as ration coupons were raided, everyone agreed that it was in a worthy cause as smiles replaced frowns for the first time in years.

Sporting life

The throttles were twisted viciously, imparting wheelspin, as the tapes rose above the riders at Foxhall Stadium in May 1965. Front wheels lifted from the ground as the foursome headed for that all important first bend. Whoever reached it in the lead could control the race, leaving those trailing in his wake hoping for an error, just one tiny opening that would allow them through. As the bikes left the start the marshals turned their faces away as cinders flew from the track, covering them in a shower of sharp dust. The crowd behind the wall at each turn ducked low as the bikes sped past, showering where they stood with another deposit from the track that they carved up. The roar of the engines, the smell of burning and the harsh taste of the cinder track are all part of the sensory enjoyment of speedway. Ipswich Witches raced into action in 1951 as the sport grew in popularity, but a dip in attendances in the 1960s meant that speedway became an on and off affair. However, it recovered and has continued non stop since 1969. Following the earlier success of Colin Gooddy, Sid Clarke and Peter Moore, John Louis became one of the sensations of the 1970s as most other riders only saw the back of his leathers over the four laps to the finishing line. Other stars of that era included Tony Davey, Billy Sanders and Mike Lanham, but each spectator had a personal favourite who was particularly admired. In the late 1960s the track was moved inside a new tarmac one laid for stock car racing.

Above: Andy Nelson led his team out between the floodlight pylon and the Churchman Stand from the cricket pavilion that acted as the club changing room. Imagine the reaction of modern, cosseted superstars if they had to endure what they would regard as primitive conditions. There was not even a hook on which to hang their mobile phones or decent parking spaces outside for the Ferraris, not to mention a way through to the hospitality box for their agents. The vast majority of Andy Nelson's career took place when there was a maximum wage in force, restricting even the top players to £20 per week, at best. Some were on even less. In the summer close season it fell to just over half and created some anomalies. One international player, on the maximum during the winter, was offered the same as everybody else during the summer. When he protested that he was a better footballer than the others he was told, 'Not in the close season you're not!' It took long battles and the threat of strike action, under the leadership of the players' representative Jimmy Hill, who later became a commentator, before club chairmen gave way. Fulham's Johnny Haynes became the first £100 per week player, but even that is small beer compared to the millions generated by modern professionals each year.

Right: Right lads, listen up for the coach is going to give you some pearls of wisdom that come from a long experience of soccer guidance. First of all this round lump of leather with a lace through the holes is called a football. You put it on the mud that some people call the pitch and kick it with all your might, hopefully in the direction of another player wearing blue. Jimmy Forsyth had to keep it simple for these were just reserve team players, still finding their way as professionals. From the left, they were Wilf Hall, Roy Goulden, Reg Pickett, John Laurel, Derek Rees, Dennis Thrower, Dermot Curtis and Kenny Malcolm. To be truthful, Jimmy gave good, professional service to the club for over 20 years and was one of the new breed of coaches at the vanguard of change in English soccer. Many of his contemporaries were of the old school, merely getting players to do some running followed by a few physical jerks and then it was off to the snooker hall or dog track. They even thought that if you kept the lads away from a football during training then they would be all the more hungry for it come three o'clock on Saturday. Scotsman Jimmy played for Millwall in between the wars and eventually became the assistant trainer at the Den. He joined Ipswich in 1950 and, as a qualified masseur and physiotherapist, helped establish a fitness regime that helped the club fill its trophy cabinets until his retirement in 1971.

This cheerful band of supporters was at the back of the north stand on Portman Walk, now renamed Sir Alf Ramsey Way in honour of the only manager to have taken a side to the championship title in all three of the Football League Divisions. The appointment of Alf Ramsey as manager in succession to the successful Scott Duncan proved a shrewd move. In 1956-57 Ipswich won the Third Division (South) title, but the club really sprang to prominence when it won the Second Division in 1960-61 and the First Division Championship a year later. This last achievement meant it had qualified for the European Cup. Ipswich went out in the second round to eventual winners AC Milan after overcoming the minnows of Floriana, Malta 14-1 on aggregate on their baptism. Ramsey went on to greater glory as manager of England's 1966 World Cup winning side and was deservedly knighted the following year. His death in 1999 was a sad loss. By then soccer had been revolutionised from the game we knew in the early 1960s when these supporters were heading off to the turnstiles. The reader can be certain that the photograph was taken not long before 3 pm on a Saturday. A similar snap in this day and age could be taken at virtually any time on any day of the week, dependent upon the whims of satellite and digital television.

Below: One boy salutes the camera as play switches to the other end of the field. It serves him right if he misses some part of the vital action for there were no giant screens to play back the exciting moments as some grounds have today. In the mid 1950s he would not have been able to see it all again on 'Match of the Day', so it was important to keep focused on the game. Some of the boys in the photograph had come to the match on their own because there was no fear of football hooliganism. Portman Road was a safer place to be than crossing the street. Nor were there any ugly or obscene chants to be heard and, should anyone curse in frustration when a penalty was skied over the bar, he would soon be told to mind his language as there were children nearby. Those boys at the front who had come with their dads had been taken down to the wall half an hour before kick off and, apart from being brought a cup of steaming Bovril at half time, did not see them again until the final whistle. Dad was some rows back where he could get an elevated view secure in the knowledge that his son was perfectly safe at the front.

Above: As John Cobbold, Ipswich's chairman, commented, 'Cinderella is quite a big girl now'. The unsung no hopers from Suffolk had performed the miracle of winning the Division One title at the first time of asking. Newly promoted Town began the 1961-62 season with a whimper rather than a bang. Wise heads nodded as a goalless draw against Bolton was followed by two defeats. Relegation was not only on the cards, but was almost a certainty according to the pundits. How they were made to eat their words when four straight victories saw the team climb up the table. Yet, even by Christmas mid table security was all that appeared to be within the team's grasp. The rest of the division had not bargained for the surge that was to begin on Boxing Day. A narrow victory over Leicester heralded a run of 18 games of which only two were lost. The others looked on in disbelief as Town raced to the number one spot and held on by beating Arsenal and Aston Villa in the final games of the season. Ray Crawford and Ted Phillips were unstoppable goalscorers, netting 61 times between them. Crawford's name would feature in football folklore once more a decade later when he helped Colchester to dump grumpy Leeds out of the FA Cup. Back row: J Compton, W Baxter, A Nelson, R Bailey, J Elsworthy, L Carberry Front row: R Stephenson, R Crawford, E Phillips, D Moran, J Leadbetter.

It really was thumbs up for the Blues during the championship season of 1961-62 as the lad in the middle of those leaning over the wall was suggesting. He wore the scarf and matching bobble hat that marked out soccer supporters long before designer gear and club strips became the uniform standing on the terraces or sitting in the stands as it now has to be since the Taylor report. He or his pals probably had a rattle with them that they swung excitedly whenever Jimmy Leadbetter weaved his magic down the wing. An unlikely looking athlete, Jimmy, a former Brighton player, fooled many a fullback into thinking that this gawky looking individual was going to be a doddle to dispossess. Only when he had seen his clean pair of heels for the umpteenth time did it dawn on him that Jimmy had gained another scalp in the long line of defenders who underestimated his ability. The lads cheering on their heroes were Town supporters long before the media invented the term 'Tractor boys'. They wrapped up warm in duffel coats with those awkward toggles that were a bind to undo with frozen fingers. Some clutched autograph books in the hope that one of the stars would scribble his name down for them. Any duplicated signatures could be used for bartering in the school playground on Monday. One Roy Bailey was worth at least three conkers.

Right: After Alf Ramsey left the club to lead the England team in its preparations for the eventual successful assault on the 1966 World Cup, Jackie Milburn took over the managerial reins. His track record as a manager did not match his playing ability as a household name for Newcastle United and Ipswich was relegated to the Second Division at the end of the 1963-64 season. The club has a fine tradition of standing by its employees when others kick out the man in charge of team affairs as soon as there is the slightest dip in form. However, it was Milburn himself who realised that he was not up to the task and he fell on his sword, paving the way for Bill McGarry to move from Watford and take control at Portman Road. Under his guidance Town regained its Division One status in 1967-68. That prompted another celebratory outburst as the boys took an open topped ride along Tavern Street. Sammy Chung and Chairman John Cobbold sat behind Bobby Hunt, Colin Harper, and Mick McNeil while other players waved to the crowd and goalie Ken Hancock showed off the trophy from the front of the bus. Cyril Lea was the chap with a hand to his mouth and he had a few months in charge of the team during the winter of 1968-69. In November 1968 McGarry decided that his interests would be better served at Wolves, but every cloud has a silver lining. After Lea's caretaker spell Bobby Robson was offered the manager's job, leading to a successful 13 year partnership with the club.

Below: It was no wonder that not an inch of spare space could be found on the Cornhill as one of the sensations of soccer history was honoured by a reception in the Town Hall. But, first of all, the team had to make its way through the seething masses to receive the official thanks of the town's dignitaries. Dressed in matching club suits, the players had already toured the town in the team bus and now posed for photographs on the edge of the multitude, trophy raised high in triumph. On Monday 14 May 1962 Ipswich Town fans roared their appreciation for the men who had achieved the near impossible feat of lifting the Division One championship. Small town teams were not supposed to be able to compete with the might of the big city clubs such as Spurs, Everton or Manchester United. Two years earlier a modest Lancashire side from Burnley showed that it was possible when it defied the big boys, but Town's success was even more remarkable as this was its first season in the top flight, having begun the campaign back in August as one of the favourites for relegation. Within just over a year Alf Ramsey's men had come from visiting such outposts as Lincoln, Leyton Orient and Rotherham to stand on the threshold of European Cup competition with the likes of AC Milan.

Below: The team bus carrying the triumphant Division Two champions along Tavern Street had just passed John Collier, the 'window to watch' as TV adverts of the time advised us. Had the boys been kitted out in their club suits there or in one of the other major clothing stores in town? In 1968 it was too soon for footballers to be demanding Versace to dress them, though a few might have cast a thoughtful eye towards London's Carnaby Street. Ipswich Town returned to the top strata of English soccer by winning the Second Division title after an epic battle with QPR and Blackpool with just a single point covering the three contenders at the finish. As usual it was Ray Crawford's goals that helped pave the way and it was fitting that he should score both the first and last goals in that season's campaign. Town had made life difficult for itself by failing to turn promising situations into outright victories. Only five games were lost, four fewer than the side in second place, but so many games were drawn that the final outcome was in doubt right up to the very end. On returning to the top division to take on the likes of Liverpool, Manchester City and Leeds our local heroes acquitted themselves well, staying in the big time for nearly 20 years in a spell that saw them come close to the League title on several occasions.

The Cornhill was just a mass of seething humanity the day they brought the First Division championship trophy home. A large V for victory in front of Grimwade's signalled the remarkable success of a club that had come straight up from the division below to take the top flight by storm. Spectators who had, just a few years earlier, gone to away matches at Aldershot, Exeter and Gillingham were now able to say that they had watched the Blues take on Bobby Charlton at Manchester United, Dave Mackay at Spurs or Gerry Hitchens at Aston Villa. Ipswich had only been a member of the Football League since the season before the war, starting off in the Third Division South. Yet here they were, riding high above some of the most famous names in soccer. Hans Christian Andersen could not have written a better fairy tale for this was a true rags to riches story of success that captured the nation's imagination. Everyone loves the underdog and Ipswich gained many friends as the big city boys were humbled week in and week out. How well the team and club staff deserved the plaudits that rained down upon their heads and the huge roar of welcome that greeted their arrival in front of the Town Hall. Even the reserved Alf Ramsey managed a smile.

Above: Somehow a little knot of schoolboys had managed to get a privileged position in front of the crush barriers holding back the crowds celebrating the best team in England. The moment that the 1961-62 team appeared on the steps in front of the Town Hall the boys' rattles would swing into noisy action, backed by the sound of baying celebration from the throats of thousands who thronged the Cornhill to pay homage to their heroes. Such heady success would have seemed light years away in the mid 1950s as Ipswich tumbled from the Second Division back down to the basement. In 1953-54 the supporters were more optimistic when the Third Division South trophy was hoisted high, but a miserable 1954-55 changed laughter into tears. However, under the guidance of Alf Ramsey, Town soon regained its earlier status, capping it with the meteoric rise to the very pinnacle of English football. The top teams today use a rotational system, resting players from time to time. There was no such idea around 40 years ago and the manager picked his best XI week in, week out. Three men, Nelson, Carberry and Moran played in each of the 42 League games, four others only missed one and two more just a couple each. All that was in addition to FA Cup and League Cup matches.

On the move

I t would be untrue to suggest that the driver
had been trying out the product being
advertised on the front of the trolley bus,
but something caused him to flip the vehicle
on its side, even if it was not a slug of Gordon's
gin. Is there something in the human nature that
draws us to a scene of disaster and then makes us
stand around gawping at the incident. It is not as
if anyone is lending a hand, for each one is
merely getting some entertainment from
another's misfortune. It is just the same on a
modern motorway when drivers slow down and
rubberneck at the carnage on the opposite
carriageway, oblivious to the dangers they are
creating on their own side of the crash barrier by
losing concentration. Perhaps the Romans
enjoyed the same sensation when they watched
the gladiators being accosted by snarling lions.
This scene of interest to the ghoulish occurred in
June 1955 when a No 109 trolley bus was travelling down Bishop's Hill on a road made greasy by
a downpour of rain. Although there were no
fatalities, several passengers needed hospital
treatment for some nasty injuries. All the houses
in the photograph are just a distant memory now,
having gone to that great terrace in the sky when
road improvements were carried out.

Left: The weather was miserable in Christchurch Park, but that did not stop the celebratory fun. All manufacturers of goods that could forge a link with the Coronation had more than one field day in 1953 as companies churned out tea towels, plates, mugs, pencils, flags and every imaginable item in red, white and blue to cash in on the event. There was even one butcher who claimed to be selling Coronation sausages, but the link with events in Westminster Abbey seemed tenuous to say the least. At home mantelpieces were adorned with the Coronation mugs, bearing the image of Her Majesty, that the children brought home from school along with their presentation cases containing a shiny five shilling crown piece. The Tolly brewery had its own beano with a celebration brew that it hoped drinkers would quaff in large quantities as they raised their glasses to the Queen on 2 June 1953. Tolly's was one of the town's two major breweries in the town centre, carrying out its business behind where Woolworth's now stands. In 1844 there were 18 maltsters and 6 brewers in Ipswich, a number that had doubled within 10 years, rising to over 300 in the borough by 1893. Three of the sons of Lord Tollemache, First Baron of Helmingham, bought out Cullingham's in 1888 and developed the business as a major rival to Cobbold's until the breweries merged in the mid 1950s.

Below: Any young reader who thinks that Footman's was a little family business that once had a shop in the town centre need only look at this photograph of the company's fleet of vehicles to take in the size of its business. Even if the lead lorry is not quite as mammoth as the modern juggernauts that blight our 21st century roads this one was big enough for the 1930s. With a little imagination you could put it onto a 1970 American interstate freeway and have it chasing Dennis Weaver in 'Duel', one of Steven Spielberg's first movies. These trucks, seen at Heath End on the edge of town, serviced most of Suffolk and parts of Essex, delivering furniture and goods ordered from the department store that stood on Westgate Street, overlooking the Cornhill. Visitors to Footman's could spend their time just browsing through its departments and floors happily enjoying the experience without purchasing anything. No excursion to Ipswich was complete without a few moments spent inside the walls of one of East Anglia's top stores. Older shoppers might remember paying for their items and then seeing their money whizzing through the air in little tubes on a track that took them to the cashier. Moments later the missile made the return journey with your change and a receipt. Tills had bells that rang a little bell when they were opened and prices popped up on little flags in the cash register window. There was not a swipe card or piece of plastic in sight.

Trolley buses, with their pantograph arms greedily sucking electricity from the overhead cables like vampire bats slaking their blood thirst, were a common feature on our roads for 40 years. These vehicles, two of which can be seen on Fore Hamlet from the bottom of Bishop's Hill, were part of a mode of transport that gradually replaced the trams during the mid 1920s. The first horse drawn trams rattled into use in 1880, running from the railway station to the Cornhill. The inaugural run carried the mayor and town clerk who claimed their seats as perks of their office. The new form of public transport was unpopular with cabbies who operated horse and carriage businesses and these men took unashamed delight when that first tram journey ended with red faces all round as it jumped the tracks. It was said the cabbies' laughter could be heard as far away as Martlesham Heath, though that might just have been an ever so slight exaggeration! Unfortunately, their mirth was shortlived and the trams flourished, especially when the Corporation gained the authority to use electricity. By 1900 electrification of the tram network was under way and the last horse drawn tram fare was paid in 1903. Their demise two decades later was tempered by the introduction of the more flexible and smoother riding trolley buses. Nearly all these buildings along Fore Hamlet have also disappeared in the wake of progress.

Above: Modern inhabitants of Ipswich can now get along swimmingly in this section of Crown Street because this is where the aquatic complex known as Crown Pools is now situated. If visitors to the town care to look up to their left when travelling along this road from the junction with Northgate Street, an out of date message is still in evidence on the gable end of one building advising you that you are 100 yards away from Egerton's. This was one of the town's major car dealers and service centres. On 11 March 1960 the company marked its golden jubilee with what it called a parade of vintage cars, though not all were legitimately true to that description. However, few bothered to nitpick about the technicality of the language, preferring to enjoy the sight of vehicles that were lined up as a representation of the changing face of motoring over the preceding 50 years. It was one that was largely British for the invasion from the Far East and other parts of Europe had not yet had the effect of decimating our own car industry. That would begin in the 1970s, though those who had a crystal ball might just have been able to prophesy what was to happen for had we not lost out to cheap imports that had started to kill off our textile industries?

Left: So there you have it. This is definitely the last trolley bus all ready to make its way from Tower Ramparts to the depot at Priory Heath in August 1963, because it says so on the front. In that case what is the one waiting behind? On closer inspection we realise that it is, in fact, a motor bus. The little lad chatting with the conductor was not too bothered about which was which as he was after getting the end of the ticket roll that boys loved to collect for some reason. Take note of his legs because he was brought up in a time of scabbed knees and wrinkled socks. Collecting ticket rolls was only one of the joys of taking a bus ride because there were other jolly things to be done. The digits on a bus ticket could be added up and converted into a message that caused teasing and hoots of laughter. A total of 12 equalled 'big, fat pig' whilst 16 meant 'I love Annie Jones', both statements being hotly denied. The top deck on the bus was the perfect place to steal someone's schoolcap and dangle it out of the window as the poor owner, usually several inches shorter than yourself, begged for its return. Another good hoot was to lean ever so quietly forward and carefully take the pigtails of the girl sitting in front. With a neat twist she could be fastened to the bar over the back of her seat and not realise that anything was amiss until she stood up in time for her stop. The squeals usually brought the conductor rushing up the stairs, by which time we had moved six rows away.

Below: The advertisers were giving conflicting messages on the trolley bus outside Egerton's garage on Crown Street. The Co-op wanted you to say its name and save money whilst Gordon's wanted its firm on your lips and its product down your throat. The passengers on board were more interested in getting to their destination than in any trite messages. They were enjoying the ride on Karrier No 107, built in 1948 with a Park Royal body that carried 56 passengers. Some of these vehicles had slatted wooden seats that tended to leave a pattern on a certain part of the anatomy. Trolley buses took over most of the tram routes during the roaring 20s, but their progress along the road was a lot less noisy than the description afforded to the decade of their introduction. Some people regarded them as a safety hazard because of their quiet approach. Trams had been much noisier, clanking their way along the tracks, but trolley buses seemed to drift along their journey with not much more than a swish. From time to time sparks and crackles came from the overhead cabling, but their usual movement was so stealthy that unwary pedestrians sometimes did not hear them coming. The unwary or careless ones stepped out into the road without looking and became an accident statistic. Some dubbed trolley buses the 'creeping death'.

On 5 July 1963 traffic was being stopped on London Road so that a survey could be carried out to help town planners with their ideas on road improvements and traffic flow. The increase in car ownership and the volume of vehicles on the road was causing congestion in the town centre and on its access roads. Drivers were asked a number of questions relating to their destinations and the timing and frequency of their journeys. Imagine attempting to conduct a survey in the same fashion at this spot in the 21st century. West End Road, to the left, and Yarmouth Road, to the right, are part of the outer ring road that also connects with the route to Felixstowe. London Road is one of the main access roads to and from the town with the fast moving A14. Any small hold up immediately creates a tail back, so men with clipboards and questions about traffic movement would create such havoc today as to snarl up the whole of this black spot with a queue that would take a few minutes to form but hours to clear. No doubt the driver of the Austin, a 60s version of white van man, would have had a few choice remarks to make if he had been stopped here some 40 years later.

Above: The day that the rains came down, though that could be any of dozens in a typical British year. On this occasion it was at the height of what was supposed to be summer in July 1963. Cliff Richard might well have been singing 'We're all going on a summer holiday' as he and his pals piled onto the bus that took Una Stubbs, Lauri Peters and Melvyn Hayes off on their travels, but we were stuck on the east coast mopping up again, just as we had in 1939 and 1953. Everything in this photograph has since disappeared from view, though it was the coming of the new road system that included the Civic Drive-Franciscan Way roundabout on Princes Street that caused the damage. This spot, being fairly close to the river, was always prone to flooding and the line of vehicles travelling bumper to bumper towards the town centre had to be wary of getting water in their distributors or the drivers would have to roll up their trouser legs. At least they could have popped in for a pint of Tolly's at the Friars whilst they waited for it all to dry out. That would have made them more relaxed than the pint and a half of milk in every bar being advertised on the billboard for Cadbury's Dairy Milk.

Shopping spree

L ooking down upon the Cornhill in 1959 the photographer might have had chance to reflect on the changes in lifestyle he had witnessed during the decade. It had begun with a Labour government that had swept to power at the end of the war, offering hope to a ravaged country. By 1951 the country had tired of waiting for the social revolution to put more money into pay packets or a ready supply of food on the shelves. In 1951 the nation turned to Churchill once again. The Conservatives stayed in charge for the rest of the 50s under a succession of prime ministers and through the problems in Korea, Cyprus, Kenya and Malaya. They rode out the Suez crisis of 1956 and, by the time the single decker bus had turned the corner into Princes Street, the economy had taken its own turn for the better. Unemployment was low and workers had money to spend on labour saving devices in the home and on entertainment for their families. Newly weds bought the washing machines and televisions that their parents had thought of as luxury goods. There was enough cash in their pockets to pay for a visit to Manning's Bar or the Golden Lion Hotel. This latter pub had been the main drinking house for commercial travellers driving their ponies and traps in the 19th century and had links dating back to 1579. In the 1960s its Vaults Bar was popular with newly affluent young people.

This picture of Westgate Street is from an era different from the one we live in now. That is obvious from the traffic on the road, the trolley bus wires, the car registration plates and the names on the shops that date this scene as being from the 1950s. But, as you look towards the Cornhill in the distance, there is a social clue given by the line of bicycles parked along the kerb on the right. In terms of technology they look dated, with their Sturmey Archer three-geared mechanism or early drop handled racing lines, but there is something not in the picture that gives the game away. There are no padlocks in sight, no chains wrapped around them and fastening them tight to a lamppost or railing. Those bikes would not last five minutes if left unattended on any modern street, never mind a town centre. How sad it is that we have become a nation fearful of walking the streets at night or of leaving our possessions unattended. What would you give for a return to the days when you left your back door unlocked in case a friend happened to call by? It seems that the richer we get the more we want and there is a large minority in society that does not care how it acquires it.

Above: As Christmas approached in 1966 children shed a tear for the passing of Walt Disney, inventor of Mickey Mouse, the manic Donald Duck, Goofy and Pluto. They did not mourn for too long as they had other interests to take their minds off the sad event. Children were being courted as mini adults by the advertising moguls, encouraged to spend their pocket money on Rolling Stones records, Carnaby Street gear and anything determined as 'cool' or 'fab'. Changes on the Ipswich skyline were on the way as well. St Matthew's Street from Westgate Street in December 1966, with Lady Lane to the left and a sighting of Albion House, included the area that was redeveloped in the late 60s and early 70s. This was despite the fact that some of the buildings that fell under the tracks of the developer's bulldozers were not that old in themselves. It had been as far back as 1951 that a plan had identified a site south of St Matthew's Street and Westgate Street for a new Civic Centre, with a police station and law courts. However, work on any of the land earmarked for this had not been commenced until 1965 when the dual carriageway of Civic Drive and Franciscan Way started to take shape.

Above: The construction of Civic Drive tolled the death knell for these buildings on St Matthew's Street and a piece of 1950s history was swept away with them. The Milk Bar was a cheap and cheerful type of café that, as its name indicated, sold non alcoholic refreshments. Most towns had them and they were places where teenagers often used to meet for a bit of peace and quiet away from the prying eyes of their parents. As time passed they evolved into coffee bars with their frothy brew gushing from steaming pipes that seemed so chic and trendy to young people who had spent their childhood in the drab years of postwar Britain. Skiffle music, with its homemade style of instrumentation of washboards and tea chest basses, had its root in these places. As that fad passed the new music of the rock era could be heard on the juke boxes, encouraging some precocious girls to swirl their long petticoats as they jived to the sounds of Eddie Cochran until the proprietor told them to sit down. The Queen's Head across the road served a stronger beverage than the Milk Bar. It had a history going back to 1680 when it was a private house, becoming a hostelry in the 18th century when cock fighting rather than dominoes and darts took place in the back room.

Above right: The baby Austin bowling along Westgate towards Museum Street in January 1956 had passed the Public Hall on the right, a building that had lain empty for years after a fire in the late 1940s. Today the building line is still very much the same as it was, even if the businesses have changed and the cars and trolley buses taken away as the whole stretch of road down to Major's Corner became pedestrianised. Although Dorothy Perkins is a name still of importance to 21st century shoppers, small hairdressing saloons, such as Ennal's, underwent major changes in the 1970s

as unisex made an impact. Barbers' striped poles largely disappeared from the street and a short back and sides, with a blob of Brylcreem on top to add a gloss, was relegated to being a thing of the past. Telling which twin had the Toni perm became applicable to both sexes! Back in the mid 50s any man entering a ladies' salon would have received short shrift as some form of oddity but, a couple of decades later, his grown up sons would think nothing of having their hair longer than that of their wives or sitting under a dryer as they waited for a frizzy perm to take hold. Before this summer was out the car driver would have been casting an anxious eye across to the Suez Canal where political problems with Egypt reached crisis levels and petrol supplies were threatened as we faced a return to the days of rationing once more.

Above: The Cornhill has always been a busy place, though in the early 1960s you could bring your car into this part of town without incurring the wrath of traffic wardens. Even so, the writing was on the wall as no entry signs, one way systems and no parking areas had already begun to make their mark. This area had long been the commercial heart of the town and, even back in Saxon days, the centre of Ipswich's activity. Some of the latter was of the brutal variety as public executions were carried out here, including nine people burnt at the stake in the 16th century. Errant locals were also put into the stocks on the Cornhill and subjected to public humiliation when insults and more hurtful things were hurled at them. There might be a case to be argued for their return for football hooligans and alcopop louts of the 21st century, but the European Court of Human Rights might have something to say about such procedures. It usually does. In the 17th century the Witchfinder General, Matthew Hopkins, indulged himself to some tune, executing no fewer than 60 Suffolk witches. When this photograph was taken we still had capital punishment in Britain, but the swinging 60s saw the last murderer swing in this fashion as the government abolished the death penalty at the end of 1964.

Right: Butter Market in the late 1950s and early 1960s was just like most of Ipswich's town centre streets, open to traffic and starting to become congested with parked cars and vehicles slowly negotiating the narrow streets. Men still went into town wearing suits and women all carried their ubiquitous large handbags. The whole area is now pedestrianised to give greater safety and comfort to shoppers. Barratt's jewellers is no longer on the corner with St Stephen's Lane, though the same trade is carried on there today by JG Andrews. Ancient House, on the opposite side of the lane, was a bookshop in this photograph and is now occupied by Lakeland Ltd. It is one of Ipswich's top landmarks and attractions, dating back to the 15th century. The Grade I listed building has been adapted to a variety of uses over its life and provides signs of perhaps six earlier buildings. For most of its existence the house belonged to the Sparrowe family and many believe that Charles II hid here after his defeat at Worcester in 1651. Panels in the ornate plasterwork represent the four continents known to man in the 17th century. Australia is missing as Captain Cook had not yet set sail and we still had room for our convicts at home.

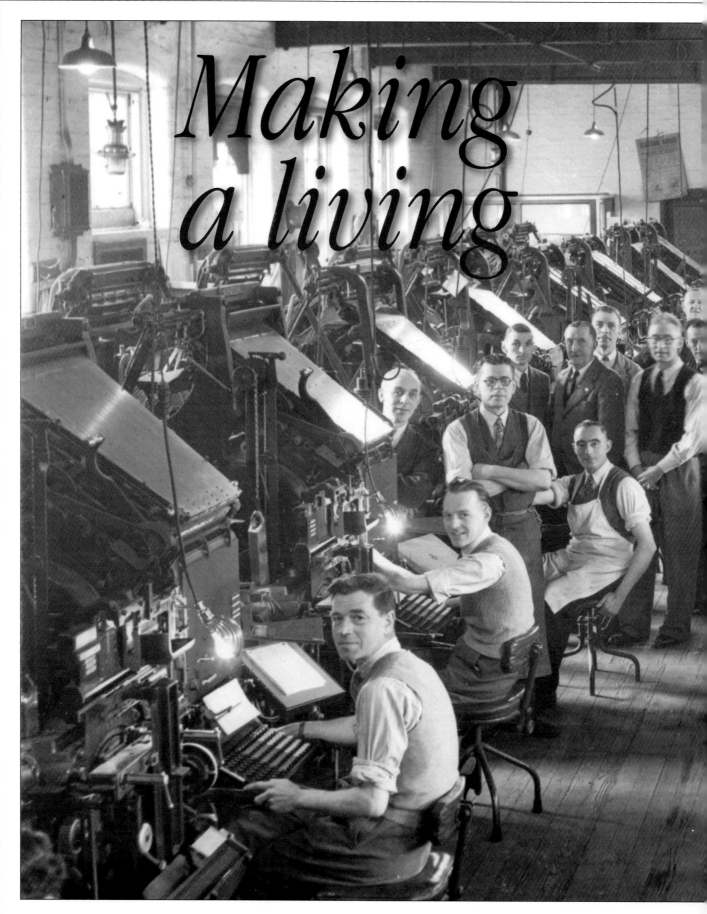

Making a living

These were the men charged with bringing you the news in the 1950s, setting up the copy in the composing room for the East Anglian Daily Times on their Linotype machines. The Carr Street offices also published the Evening Star, Mercury and Football Star, but after the area's redevelopment moved base to Lower Brook Street in May 1966, just in time to start the countdown to Alf Ramsey and the England squad's preparations for the World Cup. During the era when this photograph was taken our success on the soccer field was modest, to say the least. In 1950 baseball playing America humbled us in the World Cup and we did little better in the 1954 and 1958 campaigns. In the meantime the Hungarians had been to Wembley where the galloping major, Ferenc Puskas, and the Hungarian national side taught us a lesson. The men in the composing room had plenty of work to keep them busy during that decade, helping to reflect how things in the outside world were changing. It was not only in soccer that we ceased to reign supreme. Russia and America were now the world's super powers and we were just piggy in the middle. There were also rumblings in the Far East as China flexed her muscles and we began to worry as much about the bamboo curtain as we did about the iron one to which Churchill first referred.

Above: Down near the docks the No 2 shop in the Orwell Works that belonged to Ransome, Sims and Jefferies was getting back to production designed to meet Britain's peacetime needs. It is obvious from the clothing the men wore as to which ones were the gaffers and which got their hands dirty. On 22 October 1945 the 30,000th Motrac plough had been completed, helping to remind us that Ipswich was the county town of a significant farming area. The family business had long been associated with the manufacture of agricultural machinery, beginning with the humblest of ploughshares through to steam powered threshing machines and then modern combine harvesters. Along the way it also introduced the concept of the mechanical lawn mower at the start of the Victorian era. Robert Ransome, the company's founder, was a Quaker and his descendants followed the traditions of inter marital business connections via Quaker families. One of his great granddaughters married William Sims and, in 1865, John Jefferies married another Ransome family member. Each time another surname joined the business it was added to the company name, but the firm rationalised this complicated arrangement in 1884 when it finally settled on Ransome, Sims and Jefferies. The firm was also heavily involved in the early development of the railway system, manufacturing components and helping with the building of bridges and stations.

Merchants, traders and dealers first began wheeling and dealing on the floor of the Corn Exchange in 1882 and their successors continued to do so until June 1972. Over the next three years it was converted into an arts, conference and entertainment centre before being officially reopened as such by the Duke and Duchess of Gloucester in September 1975. Pictured on 26 February 1957, the activity was very much a male empire, reminiscent of attitudes in business that have never been fully broken down. Despite the bra burning of the late 60s and 70s eyebrows are still raised whenever an accountant, broker or scrip dealer turns out to be a woman. The Corn Exchange building was also used as a market before that moved to the troubled Greyfriars site that was itself redeveloped in the 1980s. The Corn Exchange stands just off the Cornhill, that centre of Ipswich life since early Saxon times that has played host to markets, meetings, fairs and ceremonial gatherings. From 1868 it was also home to Ipswich Town Hall. However, the Corn Exchange was always a place of practicality rather than ceremony and, even in this postwar scene, the likes of Ladbrook and Son, Cooke's and AW Green were more interested in agreeing a good price as corn merchants than in any philosophical debate in the council chamber.

Never mind the tailor's to the right, if these chaps are not careful they will be going for a burton of a different variety. For this pair, engineering technology in the 1950s was limited to a hammer and a hacksaw. 'When I nod my head, Harry, just hit it.' The health and safety executive of today will now be turning purple with apoplexy as it looks at this photograph of remedial work being carried out on the roof of the Town Hall. The decorative vases had become unstable and were having to be removed. The authorities were worried that they might fall upon unsuspecting passers by, but still allowed the work to be carried out whilst mums wheeled prams underneath, oblivious to what was happening above their heads. Nowadays there would be railings, covered ways, scaffolding and keep out signs by the score. The workmen's attire would raise more than an eyebrow on the modern inspectorate and a stop notice immediately issued unless the flat hats were removed and replaced by hard ones, though they were hardly likely to drop the vase on their own heads, now were they? Industrial gloves, boots with steel toecaps and goggles would complete the ensemble for men who only knew that the full Monty meant a new suit from Burton's and not something about prancing on a stage with nothing on.

Below: During World War II when the men went off to fight the wheels of industry just had to keep on turning. The nation's stocks had to be maintained and resources made available for those at the front. Women rallied to the cause, taking on the jobs that had traditionally been reserved for men. To augment the ranks of volunteers, part-time work became compulsory for women of 18 to 45. They ploughed the fields, harvested the crops, drove buses and flexed their muscles in engineering plants. These women worked at Ransome, Sims and Jefferies and were photographed near the gasworks in 1943. By this stage of the war Britain could see the light at the end of the tunnel, though Churchill reminded us after the victory at El Alamein in late 1942 that this was 'not the end nor the beginning of the end, but the end of the beginning'. Optimism rose during 1943 as the Germans' assault on Russia foundered, the North Africa campaign continued well, the dams in the Ruhr valley were breached and the Allies landed in Sicily. Even the church bells, once reserved for sounding a warning of invasion, could ring out again on Sundays. In Coventry, a city wrecked by bombing, a radio announcer accompanied the sound of cathedral bells being broadcast with the cry, 'Can you hear that in Germany?'

Below: It had been some years since horses dominated the roads in and around the town but it had taken until 17 November 1961 for the council to remove the last of the drinking troughs that stood on the corner of Portman Road and Princes Street. The workmen cast a careful eye over the operation because they did not want to snag the trolley bus wires that snaked overhead. After much 'to me George, to you Albert' one of the last links with the Victorian era was hoisted safely onto the back of the lorry and taken away as just so much impedimenta of yesteryear. Perhaps it was a sight like this that the following summer encouraged Bernard Cribbins to sing 'Right said Fred', his amusing ditty about he and Charlie struggling with an unidentified object before having another cup of tea and going home. As usual a couple of passers-by had stopped in the hope that some calamity would overtake the crane and that the whole operation would end in a heap on the floor, but these chaps were equal to the task and the trough was up and away without a problem. The gaffer giving directions took most of the credit for the successful conclusion, even if he never got his hands dirty in the process.

This is the price of progress. Huge scars cut across the history of streets that had been trodden by Thomas Wolsey, Robert Sparrowe, Thomas Gainsborough and even Sir Alf Ramsey. St Matthew's Street was laid waste as the needs of motorists and commerce demanded road widening to relieve congestion and create a more user friendly town centre where shoppers could move more freely. St Matthew's Baths Hall, in the centre, was used as a swimming pool in the summer and boarded over as a function room in the winter. Although one of the main aims of the new road system of roundabouts, Civic Drive and a free flowing ring road system around the centre was intended to aid the flow of motor vehicles, it became self defeating. More and more cars were attracted to use the highways and, before too long, congestion was just as severe as ever. The motorist then became the target of both local and national government, the leper who had to be provided with a colony on the outskirts known as park and ride. Town centre car parks were only for those capable of surviving the wallet equivalent of a blood transfusion each time they stumped up the parking fee. Those filling up their tanks in the 1960s to the sound of 'the Esso sign means happy motoring' could have written new and ruder lyrics to the slogan by the end of the century.

It was late June 1961 when these men started to put up the garlands on Fore Street that would be part of the visual greetings to welcome Queen Elizabeth II to town. It took one man up a ladder, two to feed the decoration from the corn flake box and one to direct operations before this simple task could be achieved. This probably helped to inspire a generation of time and motion experts to descend upon the shop floors of industry. By Pass Nurseries had provided the flowers and greenery and must have wished for many more royal visits to bolster trade. The Martin and Newby van belonged to the ironmongery firm that still trades today from within part of the premises that were once the old Bull's Head public house. The lorry parked in front of the By Pass vehicle belonged to Smyth Brothers, another local ironmonger's. Behind it were a stationer's, Porter and Tonkin Ltd and Rapid Radio. The name of the electrical service company reminds us that the old wireless was still a favourite source of family entertainment, but it was in its last years as a serious rival to television. By this time most homes had a goggle box and before long radio would become little more than a vehicle for music, though fans of 'The Archers' might argue with that description.

A driving force in Ipswich for over 80 years!

Not many folk use the word 'chara' these days. If you still use it then its a sure sign that you're getting a bit long in the tooth. For younger readers who may be wondering what on Earth a chara might be we should explain that it is short for charabanc. But even after that explanation we'd guess that most youngsters will still have blank looks on their faces. We'd better come clean and admit that it's old folks' slang for a coach, a motor coach that is not a stagecoach, we're not that old!

Modern motor coaches tend to look very similar to single decker buses though often with many more facilities, but the charabanc was quite different. The French word meant literally a carriage with benches and in a sense that is exactly what they were. The original charas were in fact horse drawn, but imagine a very long open topped car with several rows of bench seats and that was the original motor chara; they would become a familiar sight in the 1920s taking day trippers to destinations everywhere. The only drawback to the chara was that although there was a hood there were no windows and the sides remained open to the elements no matter what the weather.

Charas may have disappeared into history quite quickly after a brief period of being in vogue, though the name would survive for many decades after their demise. Even in the 1960s people still spoke of charas when they meant motor coaches without giving the word a second thought. We are all familiar with motor coaches these days, and with coach tours, but still just within living memory they were a novelty. Tourists

Above: Founder Mr Albert Soames.
Right: Albert (son of the founder) with brother-in-law Frank. *Below:* An early Soames coach.

however had been making day trips by train ever since Thomas Cook organised the first package trips quite early in the 19th century when he sent organised groups by train to religious meetings; but road transport was quite a different matter. The internal combustion engine and good metalled roads came many decades after the railways. Though motor vehicles were around at the end of the 19th century it was to be the period of the first world war which saw millions of motor vehicles appear; following the war many of the vast engineering plants designed to meet war production were turned over to car production. And the massive increase in the number of cars which resulted, in turn created a demand for better, faster roads. Before long journeys which had once been impractical by road became instead a viable alternative to the railways, even if the horses and carts on them still outnumbered motors.

Into that expanding arena were drawn a number of individuals who saw the potential for providing coach and bus services making use of both the new vehicles which were finding their way on to the market and the ever improving roads on which they might travel. One such individual was the founder of local coach firm A Soames & Sons.

Today the owners of the company are Anthony Soames, his son Andrew and daughter Mandy.

The firm was founded however in Clopton by Albert Soames, the present owners' grandfather and great-grandfather, around 1920 after an earlier career driving a hawker's van from which he sold food, baskets, pots, pans and paraffin.

Albert was helped by his sons Albert and Ken; and their respective sons, Anthony and Michael, who would, in turn, eventually join the firm too.

During the war Albert Soames senior continued to run the business whilst his sons served in the forces. The business

stayed based at Clopton until around 1949 when it moved to its present base in Chapel Road, Otley.

How many thousands of our readers have travelled on a Soames' coach we wonder over the decades since the founder bought his first vehicle? Tens, probably hundreds of thousands we would guess who would make up millions of passenger journeys between them. Whether today's air conditioned high rise coaches are as good as those of the days of our youth we can't say; certainly the latest coaches

Top left: Albert pictured with daughter Jacqueline.
Top right: A bell ringing tour to Cheddar Gorge. Above: A Soames Ford from the 1960s.
Right: Glady's on tour with daughter Jacqueline.

coach trip these days that provides the driver with the dubious pleasure of listening for the umpteenth time to the seemingly endless verses of 'Ten Green Bottles' let alone a complete repertoire from setting off to arriving back home. And do coaches make emergency stops in lay-bys to enable passengers to run behind the hedgerows for an impromptu 'comfort break'? Maybe not now with the advent of luxury coaches equipped with en suite facilities for long journeys; of course it's better really, but there's got to be a lot less laughter than there used to be.

Today A Soames & Sons Ltd's main business comes from providing daily school transport, contract and private hire, tours for both travel companies and private hire including day trips and tours to Europe. Main customers include Suffolk County Council, Ipswich High School for Girls, independent school bus clubs and the Travelstyle tour company.

Mandy and Andrew Soames are the fourth generation of the family to work in the firm and are hoping to continue the traditions set by their great grandfather and use the company's experience, local knowledge and reputation for reliability.

Perhaps over the other side of the English Channel French folk still refer to a coach as a chara; we don't know if they do but amongst the older generation here, some of us at least will continue with that old name for a few years yet.

go much faster, except when they are stuck in traffic jams, and the seats are probably more comfortable and the air less likely to be filled with Woodbine smoke - from the driver as much as the passengers but... Well do the passengers enjoy their trips as much as we did in yesteryear? Back then any kind of a trip was an adventure, especially in the days when so few of us owned our own cars. Coaches provided a form of luxury transport far removed from the local bus with their almost exotic orange roof panels and the exciting chance to be able to actually sit next to the driver, an opportunity never offered on a bus. And whatever happened to community singing we wonder? It's a rare

Top left: *One of the A Soames & Sons fleet taking part in the procession to greet Ipswich Towns first division championship winning team of 1962.* ***Above:*** *Melton Youth Club Old Boys FC on a trip to Ostend, Anthony (present owner) fifth from the right, his late wife Janet second from the right.* ***Right:*** *The company premises pictured in 1971.*

Lock stock and two useful sons

We may think we know all about ironmongery, but where do the building trade get all their bits of ironmongery from. One answer is Ipswich's Lister Locks Ltd.

The company was founded on 6th May 1974 by David Lister, known to all as 'JDL'.

In 1957, long before starting the firm, JDL had joined a London tool wholesale business based in the City of London and which later relocated to Greenhithe in Kent. That businesses expanded through acquiring a small ironmongery wholesaler and then outgrew its premises and decided in 1973 to restructure the firm by demerging. In 1974 JDL took the opportunity to return home to Suffolk by purchasing the stock and goodwill of the company's now growing lock and builders ironmongery division; JDL formed a new company, Lister Locks Ltd. The new business moved to the Farthing Road industrial estate in Ipswich.

From Farthing Road the business concentrated on stocking and distributing locks, security fittings and builders ironmongery - operating as a strictly bona fide wholesale builders merchant outlet on behalf of British manufacturers and selling only to builders merchants and DIY stores.

JDL was helped by his two sons: John who was responsible for purchasing, warehouse management and distribution and Colin, who was responsible for external sales.

It was however JDL who had the vision and the marketing expertise that provided the foundation for the firm's growth. Surprisingly the company's first computer system was installed as long ago as 1976, an investment which would be continuously renewed and updated to the present day.

Shortly after moving into Unit 17 in Farthing Road the adjacent unit became available and so the floor area was

Top left: *Founder David Lister.*
Above : *A Listers 'Listerpack'.*
Below: *Listers office and warehouse premises.*

In the years since the company moved to Landseer Road its founder David 'JDL' Lister has passed away, but his three children John Colin and their sister Catherine Girling remain as non executive directors. Today the business is headed up by Robert N Peters, Managing Director, supported by his team of directors and managers. It has developed into a national distribution centre supplying all major builders merchants across the United Kingdom with a range of locks, security fittings, fixings and architectural ironmongery. It employs more than 200 staff at its Ipswich base and has in-house production facilities for pre-packing goods and also has commercial interests in India, a source of many brass and 'black' ironmongery products.

Top left: *Listers warehouse area.*
Left: *Trained staff waiting to take orders in the company's Sales Office.*
Below: *Listers Directors, (from left to right) Steve Williams, Robert N Peters, Sheila Chambers and Tim Slingo.*

immediately doubled. In 1989 the company moved to Unit 3 which had almost three times the floor area. The business however soon absorbed even this large space and took on the lease on the adjacent warehouse before in 1992 buying Unit 12, yet another 20,000 sq. ft unit.

Growth however would be unremitting and even more space was needed. From Farthing Road the company moved across town over the Easter break of 1990 to its current site in Landseer Road. Ironically the new building had been originally developed in the late 1970s as a builders merchants outlet by another established Ipswich company, Sankey Smythe Ltd. The logistics worked, all was ready for the start of play on Tuesday and Listers would never look back.

Hard wearing hardware

One of the Ipswich area's longest established businesses must be that of ironmongers MW Partridge & Co. Ltd based at 60 High Street, Hadleigh. The showrooms on the corner of George Street look like a substantial three storey building from the outside, but a visit to the loft space above the first floor would reveal a different story. The timbers of the original steeply pitched roof rise from the 'floor'. However, a lath and plaster wall with sash windows and a shallower pitched roof have been added so as to give a more impressive appearance from the High Street, an 'improvement' which is believed to date from the Georgian period.

Astonishingly the deeds of that property confirm that there has been a continuous ironmongery business on the premises since at least 1823.

In 1823 Thomas Pritty, an ironmonger and ironfounder, acquired the property from one Charles Pretty (or perhaps Pritty), leading to the speculation that Charles, perhaps Thomas's father, had also been running a similar trade there even earlier.

Thomas Pritty ran his business from the High Street until 1861 when he sold his firm to another ironmonger and ironfounder - John Graham. By 1865 John Graham was working in partnership with a Richard Crush Joslin to whom he left the business on his death in 1883.

Sixteen years later, in 1899, Richard Joslin leased the premises for 21 years to Henry Robert Taylor for £80 per annum. Richard Joslin died in 1900 leaving the property to his wife and brother. Eight years later, after they had both died, Henry Taylor was able to buy the freehold.

Henry Taylor continued to run his business until 1929, when he sold out to two partners, the delightfully named Maitland Walter Partridge of Hadleigh, (after whom the present business takes its name) and Daniel Partridge of Kersey. Accounts from the first years of trading still exist. In the first eight months of business

*Above: Partridge & Partridge accounting documents dated 1931. **Below:** Maitland Walter Partridge, circa 1929. **Inset:** M W Partridge & Co. Ltd, 2000.*

grates was a major part of Partridges' service during this period along with fitting new fire bars and flue pipes which were made in the workshop and the forge, alongside sheet metal work. Typical work recalled during this time by long time employee Eric Norman, who started work for the firm at the age of 14 in 1941, included climbing St Mary's church roof to fit flue pipes for the stoves that then heated the church.

Other employees left the firm for the duration of the second world war; Jim Hynard for example, who had joined Partridges in 1936, went to work for De Havilland as a welder on aircraft production; he came home to Polstead after the war and returned to Partridges where his skill as a welder was greatly admired

ending 31st March 1930, sales exceeded £4,000 leaving a net profit for each of the partners of almost £240. In the first full year of trading sales amounted to £7,563 18 s.4d with a net profit for each of the partners of £391.0s.9d each, perhaps not a fortune but still a tidy sum back then, before galloping inflation began to eat into the value of our money.

That early partnership did not last long. In 1934 it was dissolved and Walter Maitland Partridge and his sister Edith Partridge registered the long-lasting name of M W PARTRIDGE & CO.

One example of the type of things sold by Partridges at this time was the Hadleigh Cooking Range; these were in fact made in Scotland though sold as own brand through the 1930s and into the 1940s. An example of this Range is still on view at Edward's Hadleigh showroom, 55 High Street. The installation and maintenance of stoves and

until his retirement in 1987. Such long service with the company is not unusual, both then and now. Jim Hynard's nephew John Smyth, who started with the firm in 1958, is now Partridge's Garden and Estate machinery

Above, both pictures: *Early agricultural shows.* ***Right:*** *The Hadleigh cooking range, made in Scotland and sold as an 'own brand' in the 1930s and 1940s.*

manager, whilst his wife Gloria has worked in the accounts department since their marriage in 1964. Jim Becket, in charge of the large stock of machinery, started in 1953 and Richard Hill, still working in the spares department, joined Partridges in 1963. Richard's brother Jim Hill joined the company in 1954 and is currently manager of all departments other than machinery. Jim Beckett, Jim and Richard Hill, and John and Gloria Smyth all worked for Walter Partridge.

Despite the hard times of the 1930s and the war years, the business had prospered and in 1946, at the end of the second world war, Partridges was able to acquire Salters, the domestic hardware shop across the road at number 53, (now part of Edwards). They continued to run this

Hardware business, thus complementing the Ironmongery and Agricultural Engineering business at 60 High Street.

Obtaining supplies in the post-war years was not without its difficulties, not least supplies of paraffin. As a result Partridges formed a partnership with Stiffs of Kersey, the 'Wholesale Kerosene Company' or WKC. Paraffin was big business at the time with deliveries to surrounding villages where there were still a great many houses without electricity. Paraffin oil was used for lighting, heating and cooking in some homes. Most tractors ran on paraffin at that time; they were made with a small tank for petrol and a large tank for paraffin, after starting on petrol there was a tap to switch to paraffin as soon as the engine was hot enough.

The business became a limited company - MW Partridge & Co. Ltd - in 1949 with its managers becoming directors of the new company and forming the team that ran the company for the following thirty-five years. Harold Sexton

Above: Some of the paraffin lamps and heaters sold by the firm in the late 1940s and 50s. Left: An old advertisement for Salters. Below: From left to right, Jim Becket, Eric Norman, and Jim Hynard.

the foundry, although the roof over the door had to be raised to get them out! Later models, which came complete, including the famous 780, were sold in considerable numbers - 16 in 1956 alone. Later, however the shop's town centre position and the loss of land due to construction of Magdalen Road, would make it impossible to handle the huge farm machines which would appear later in the century, leaving Partridges to eventually concentrate more on garden and estate machinery along with DIY, hardware and ironmongery.

joined the business in 1946 after the war and worked for the firm until his death in 1968. Others served even longer: Frederick Thorpe for example joined the firm in 1931 and did not retire until 1984 at the age of 76, Frank Goymour served until the age of 71 having clocked up 44 years by the time he retired in 1984 along with Leslie Pearson, a relative youth at the age of 68 when he retired in 1984 but who had begun working for Partridges in 1929 long before farming became so highly mechanised.

Farms and machinery were smaller then and there was a lot of handwork with hoes, pitch forks, muck forks etc. greatly in demand from the farming families and farm workers, many more than exist today. Most farms and estates within a radius of ten miles would have an account with Partridges.

As agricultural engineers the 'new' company enjoyed a brisk trade throughout the 1950s as agents for heavy equipment with Massey Harris as one of the strongest brand manufacturers, providing a complete range of agricultural machinery from seed drills to combine harvesters. The first 'combines' came from the USA, by rail, to Hadleigh station and delivered to Partridges in crates. They were assembled in

Maitland Walter Partridge died in 1969 and the remaining directors inherited the business and property, which they continued to run until 1984.

Cosford Property Company bought the business in 1984 and from then on would operate it as a subsidiary whilst retaining the name of MW Partridge & Co. Ltd.

With Keith Young as the new Managing Director, all the staff, other than the directors who had retired, continued in their jobs but changes to update the business began.

At that time the property included the corner shop at 60 High Street, the house at 62 High Street, where Walter Partridge, as he was always known, had lived with his sisters Edith, Carrie, Nellie and Ruth and which had remained unoccupied since Walter's death. 1, 3 and 5 George Street, owned by the firm, had also remained empty for many years.

Top, both pictures: An early advertisement for the famous 780, as driven by George Nicholls in the photograph. **Right:** *Demonstrating a tractor sold by Partridges.* **Far right:** *W Partridge in later years.*

The first work to be put in hand was to re-roof all of these properties. They were effectively one building, various parts dating from the 14th to the 16th century. Eventually they would form a single showroom on the ground floor for the Household/Cookware/Garden departments. On the first floor would be two more showrooms - Tools/Electrical and Ironmongery/Security.

The properties had small gardens and beyond them a range of outbuildings. A concrete block workshop on the Magdalen Road frontage (still there) along with two Nissen huts and the foundry, last active in the 19th century, still referred to as such though used for agricultural machinery repairs. There were also various other store buildings of brick and wood; all except the workshop on Magdalen Road were now demolished to make way for new buildings.

Partridges owned land extending all the way to the back of the public car park on the other side of Magdalen Road, most of which was compulsorily purchased for the construction of Magdalen Road and the car park in 1971.

Partridges, however, still owned 0.4 acres at the back of the car park on which stood two 5,000-gallon oil tanks and provided space to stand machinery. The firm did not, however, own the plot on the corner of George Street/ Magdalen Road.

A deal was done with the Council to exchange these pieces of land. The Council extended the car park and Partridges was able to square off the corner plot to build new showrooms for Garden Machinery and Paint/Plumbing etc.

Paint began to feature strongly in sales and in 1989 the firm received an award from Dulux as an outstanding retailer of its goods. Today Partridges has a large paint and decorating department with Dulux still its strongest brand.

In 1989 Partridges also took over a garden machinery business from Mann Egerton in Ipswich, which included the wholesale distribution of leading brands throughout Suffolk; three of Mann Egerton's staff still remain with Partridges more than ten years later.

The start of the 1990s saw Partridges gain national publicity, and do some good for others, when it joined the Orchard Players to raise funds to provide a wheelchair for an Ipswich girl. Money was raised by a sponsored ride from John O'Groats to Land's End, a journey made on a 'ride-on' lawn tractor provided by Partridges, driven by the Orchard Players and followed by a Partridges service van driven by Partridges Kevin Leech.

Meanwhile, in Hadleigh, changes continued. A warehouse behind the showrooms and a large extension to the

Top left: Mr Jim Hynard, who started working for MW Partridge in 1936, receives a retirement gift of a watch presented to him by his nephew, Mr John Smyth, on behalf of work mates, 1987. Top right: Receiving the Outstanding Retailer Award, 1989.

Partridges became the largest shop in Hadleigh town centre with a total floor area of around 24,000 square feet, about half of which is retail showroom the rest being offices, stores and workshops.

After nearly two hundred years the business still draws custom from a wide area and remains known for its quality and its competitive pricing. Despite a shift away from agricultural supplies the firm still maintains its long standing links with farmers, supplying such items as electric fencing, shotgun cartridges and clays, hydraulic pipes and fittings, oils and other sundries, spare parts as well as small machines such as chain saws, compressors and generators. The firm also sponsors the annual Farmers Association clay pigeon shoot as well as having trade stands for many years at the Hadleigh, Tendring and Suffolk shows.

A truly remarkable record since 1823.

workshop completed the building and renovation programme around 1996.

The Salters hardware shop at 55 High Street, on the corner of Church Street, bought in 1946, though still generally known as Salters even though it traded as MW Partridge & Co. Ltd since it was acquired, was now closed with the business being incorporated into the extended main shop at 60 High Street.

By the millennium Partridges was trading as a general hardware department store, and still as an independent business; it remains unique in its wide range of stock and its knowledgeable and long serving staff.

Despite a number of retirements near the end of the 20th century, by the millennium there were still five employees who had personally worked with Walter Partridge and 22 out of the total of 39 employees had been with the company for more than ten years.

Top left: *Viewed by TV cameras, Griff Rhys-Jones wishes staff from Partridges well as they are about to embark on their charity fund raising mission to provide a wheelchair for an Ipswich girl.* **Top right:** *Promoting the fund raising mission at the Hadleigh Show.* **Above left:** *Sir Joshua Rowley (Lord Lieutenant of Suffolk) making a donation.* **Below:** *The new part of the company premises in 2001.*

Cultivating a college in the community

In times gone by those engaged in agriculture and animal husbandry could only hope to pick up the skills of their calling by learning on the job. Farmers' sons learned their trade from their fathers whilst others who had no connection with the land, but who yearned to make their living from it, had little opportunity to learn the necessary knowledge and skills they required.

That situation was gradually to change in the late 19th and early 20th centuries with the gradual appearance of a number of educational institutions which would eventually evolve into modern agricultural colleges. And moreover what was once an art would eventually become a science. Green fingers may once have been sufficient qualification for a career on the land, but no longer.

By the millennium Otley College, located six miles from Ipswich, was offering courses from Foundation level to Masters Degree in a wide variety of subjects. Originally created as an Agricultural and Horticultural College, Otley has expanded its range of courses over a number of years. With the latest facilities and a dynamic teaching and support staff, Otley has become well placed to provide individual students and company employees with the skills and knowledge needed for success in the business world.

The Otley College campus was built to replace outgrown facilities in nearby Witnesham, by the East Suffolk Institute of Agriculture, on land leased from the Felix Cobbold Agricultural Department Trust. The Agricultural Education Centre at Witnesham was opened in 1960 and ran courses in tractor maintenance, ploughing and animal and crop husbandry, amongst others. Lord Netherthorpe, Chairman of Fisons, presided over the opening of the new campus at Otley in 1970. Mr Graham Boatfield, former Agricultural Organiser for East Suffolk, was appointed as Otley's first Principal.

Above: *Tractors used for courses in Tractor maintenance and for ploughing the land (as seen in the picture below).*
Below: *Students inspect the soil after ploughing.*

support its students in their courses was confirmed with the opening of a new library and study skills centre. Steps were taken to further enhance the experiences of students with the introduction of the first European exchange programme in 1990. Within a dozen years regular partnership exchanges would be taking place with students from Portugal, Sweden, Finland, France, Spain, Belgium, the Netherlands, Hungary and Poland.

As well as reaching out to the continent, Otley College also undertook a programme of introducing Outreach Centres, to help meet the training and leisure needs of Suffolk and North Essex. Those centres, located at Leiston, Colchester, Lowestoft and Rendlesham, would offer courses from Information Technology to Floristry and Construction.

Until 1974, the only department operating at the College was that of Agriculture. In that year, the Horticultural Department was established on the site, coincidentally John W Pearson who would be Principal at the beginning of the 21st century would join the college staff in that same year. Two years later, the emblem of Otley College, the 'Black Bull' sculpture, was created by Rintoul Booth and installed beside the main entrance.

The 1980s saw existing departments extending their range of courses, while new departments opened their doors for the first time. The first full-time course in Horticulture and Environmental Studies was offered in 1980. The National Certificate in Floristry began in 1986, closely followed by the launch of the first equine course. The equine course was run in partnership with the Newton Hall Equestrian Centre, and continues to do so. The Horticultural Department was pleased to offer its first Royal Horticultural Society courses in 1988, while the Environment Management Unit Department was created in 1989 to provide Advanced National Certificate courses in Horticulture, along with Conservation and Ranger Skills courses.

That momentum was maintained in the 1990s, as the new departments of Animal Care, Construction, Sport and Recreation, IT, and a Centre of Excellence for Floristry were nurtured. Otley's commitment of resources and services to

Otley College values its friendly and informal, yet professional and dynamic, environment for learning. The College's 6,500 students, young and old, full-time and part-time, have come to rely upon the Student Advice Team for guidance and support and on the Student Committee for social activities during their time at the College. With so much to offer, Otley College prides itself on being big enough to matter, but small enough to care.

Top left: *Otley College (front).*
Top right: *The IT training room.*
Above left: *Students on their animal science course.*
Below: *Inside the college grounds.*

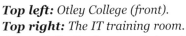

Residents of Lancing Avenue celebrate
Queen Elizabeth II's coronation in 1953.

Acknowledgments

The publishers would like to thank

David Kindred

Andrew Mitchell

Steve Ainsworth